LIFEWORK:
Portraits of Iowa Women Artists

Photographs by Robbie Steinbach
Marianne Abel, Editor
Carol Lauhon, Contributing Editor

Lifework Arts Press
Bettendorf, Iowa

Acknowledgements: Portions of the text by Laura Julier (Stensaas) first appeared in *Iowa Woman*, Vol. 13(3), Autumn 1993. Portions of "Imaging Iowa Women Artists" by Robbie Steinbach, and texts by Paddy Blackman (Illian, Wagener), and Carol Lauhon (Banks-Craighead, Schedl, Schussheim-Anderson, Steinbach) first appeared in *Iowa Woman*, Vol. 15(1/2), Spring 1995.

Library of Congress Catalog Card Number: 98-75013

Steinbach, Robbie.

Lifework: Portraits of Iowa Women Artists/ by Robbie Steinbach

p.   cm.

ISBN 0-9668048-0-5

Lifework Arts Press

Bettendorf, Iowa

Front Cover: Sarah Jane Boyd, Davenport, Iowa 1991
               Photograph by Robbie Steinbach
Back Cover: Sally Stepanek, Tipton, Iowa 1995
               Photograph by Robbie Steinbach

Book Design by Marge Myers

Printing by Fidlar Printing Co. Davenport, Iowa

This book is dedicated to my daughter Molly,
and to all our daughters - those of blood and those of spirit.
May you have creative and fulfilling lifework.

Acknowledgements

I owe the existence of this book to so many people. I thank Carol Lauhon, friend and fearless feminist and "mother" of the Now or Never Writing Class, for the marathon dance: for the benefit of her incisive intelligence during those three-hour breakfasts when we began shaping the dream, and for her ferocious caring about girls' and women's lives. I am grateful to Paddy Blackman, who enthusiastically jumped into the project upon the first asking. She traveled the state with me, braving ice storms and artists' cats, to learn about art and women's lives. Jeanne Tamisiea took on the early design, creating the first semblance of form out of chaos, and shared her vision about what it means to be an artist and a woman. Marianne Abel brought to this project not only her years of work as an editor, writer, and artist, but also her steadfast support for the creative lives of women. Her calm presence and sense of humor when most needed have proved invaluable to me. Marge Myers had taken an early retirement from the design firm she owned in order to work on her own art. But when I asked if she would take on the designing of this book, she said, "Yes, I'll do it." She has persisted in shaping the book despite pain and surgery, a new puppy, and my constantly adding new responsibilities to her job description.

I am indebted to all the essay writers who shared their many talents: Dawn Bowman, Denise Lamphier, Jean Florman, Laura Julier, Julie Jensen McDonald, Teresa Ruzic, Harriet Harmelink, and the late Kay Kehoe. The featured artists not only made themselves available as subjects, but also gave suggestions for other artists to contact, funding sources, and museums and galleries in which to show the work. The staff of the Davenport Museum of Art, with that first exhibition in 1993, provided the support of my work and other women's art that led to this book. Members of the Women's Studies Program at Augustana College did last-minute proofreading. My longtime friend, Mary Ann Moore, worked on publicity. Attorney and arts advocate Ted Priester donated his legal expertise so that Lifework Arts Foundation might be born.

I could not have completed this book without the assistance of many funders. The Iowa Arts Council and Quad City Arts granted funds for photographic materials. An anonymous Quad-Cities woman generously supported the book at two crucial junctures. The American Association of University Women of Muscatine, Iowa, sent a check after viewing my work at the Muscatine Art Center. Dr. Joseph Kehoe donated in memory of his late wife, writer Kay Kehoe. Artist Sheryl Ellinwood, The Isabel Bloom Foundation and M. C. Ginsberg also provided much-appreciated support for the project.

I treasure those friends who were present throughout this long process, encouraging me when it seemed all the pieces would never come together. Special appreciation goes to my husband Jim and daughter Molly, who took the brunt of the grousing when things weren't going as well or as quickly as I desired. I appreciate the meals they cooked and pets they tended while I was on the road, in the darkroom, or on the computer. Molly read essays and critiqued photographs when I needed an in-house opinion. Jim has supported my art for many years: building darkrooms in two homes, loading boxes of photos into cars, and hanging shows with me. My lifework is truly a collaborative venture.

—Robbie

Table of Contents

Robbie Steinbach: Self-portrait in collaboration with Laurie Elizabeth Talbot Hall , 1997

Imaging Iowa Women Artists

In 1985, I began photographing women in their homes. I wanted to make their work visible. A similar motivation led me to begin this project six years later. The work of women artists has long been underrepresented and undervalued. My collection of photographs resists the myth that successful women artists are anomalies. The Iowa women pictured here are among the many talented artists who have successful creative careers. They are strong, intelligent, determined women; women with a great sense of themselves. They are beautiful women. Their portraits defy the tradition of imaging women as beautiful objects. They are creative, not created.

When I began photographing women artists, I had just finished graduate school. I needed a project which could sustain my interest for years. I was a novice at being an artist, as I had begun serious photographic work only when I was in my late thirties. I was still trying to figure out what it meant to be an artist, and I especially felt a need to see how other women worked as artists. I was also looking for ways to make more positive images of women. As an older, non-traditional student in grad school, I had successfully fought to have my "domestic" photographs of women taken seriously. Yet I felt I had been encouraged to make photographs of women that were critical, or even belittling. Since I was still in the process of sorting out my own feelings about being a woman in our society, I occasionally fell into that trap.

Near the end of my time in graduate school, three women's responses helped change my work. A well-known visiting artist, whose own work had once dealt with the suicide of her mother, looked at my photographs of women in their homes. She said, "I'm tired of looking at depressing images of women." Another woman viewed my satirical video about a woman who strives to look like Marilyn Monroe and has a bedroom shrine dedicated to the actress. I was moved when this fellow student responded, "This woman is your sister. Why are you making fun of her?" About the same time, an artist/teaching colleague said to me, "It will be interesting to see if, when you are done with grad school, your images become more positive."

As I came to embrace feminism, and grew to better understand the cultural and societal factors that had shaped my life and the lives of other women, I became uncomfortable with some of my earlier images. I didn't feel that my photographic portraits had to be safe and sanitized or always smiling. However, I became conscious of wanting to portray not the flaws or women's "stuck" place in society, but instead the strength, individuality, intelligence and creativity of women. The artists featured in this book, although diverse in their personalities and in the kinds of art they create, share these qualities.

A project which concentrates only on women can be problematic. While most of the artists have expressed pleasure in being shown in the company of their female peers, they've also said that, ideally, gender should not be an issue. As Georgia O'Keeffe once said, "The men liked to put me down as the best woman painter. I think I'm one of the best painters."[1]

While I don't wish to contribute to placing women in a "gender ghetto," one aspect of the lives of artists who are women has intrigued me. Most of these women juggle so many roles: primary caretakers of children and the home, teacher, income-earner, etc. How do they manage to create original art as well? How does the artist stop painting to work in her office, drive her daughter to saxophone lessons, pick up some groceries, and then recapture the original energy in her studio? In her dissertation on women's creativity, C. Diane Ealy quotes psychologist Lita Linzer Schwartz: "In the realms of creativity, one would have difficulty finding anything that is more creative than the juggling of time, space, emotion and activity by the woman who is wife, mother, and worker."[2] To that list, I would add "artist."

These photographs are not only portraits of other women artists, they are my means of self-expression and my own art. I have made choices of subject, lighting, and timing. I've used black-and-white photography rather than color because of its expressive, abstract, and archival qualities. The centrality of composition I have often chosen stresses the centeredness of these strong women in their environments. I've endeavored to find fresh ways to photograph each artist, to show something unique about each woman.

When I visited an artist, she and I became co-creators. Together we selected places and activities which captured something of her personality and spirit. We seldom posed her in front of her easel or potter's wheel or loom, as is so often done in this kind of portraiture. Instead we explored other settings which are also part of her life.

I've had a grand time exploring Iowa and meeting the artists. Among many memories, a few stand out: writer Paddy Blackman and I braving an ice storm to travel to Martha Yoder's farm south of Iowa City, to be warmly greeted with tea and homemade bread. Me presenting a comical picture as, dressed in a borrowed huge bright orange slicker, I held my precious camera aloft while falling in the mud near Starla Stensaas' home in the loess hills of western Iowa. Photographing Verna Banks-Craighead as she rode her bicycle back and forth over a bridge, obliterating the obscene words someone had written in the snow. Standing on a dock over the Mississippi River, watching Sarah Jane Boyd sail away, powered only by the wind caught in a tattered paper umbrella. Cajoling Laurie Hall's puzzled teenaged daughters into hauling an old dresser into their yard, and seeing the rolling hills and the blue sky reflect in the round mirror as we moved. Feeling privileged to photograph Concetta Morales just days before she gave birth to her second child. Laughing with Mary and Kristina Young Bear and Marianne Abel as we shared stories over a lunch of soup with fry bread, strawberries, and banana cream pie. Traipsing around Bonnie Koloc's garden as she sang parts of her upcoming one-woman show, trailed by her two dogs and a cat; then sitting on her front porch overlooking the rolling hills of northeast Iowa, drinking wine and talking. I remember feeling a thrill of recognition when she said, "Art is the one thing I can always count on."

It hasn't always been easy. The weather was invariably uncooperative when I took my longer field trips. It poured rain during the entire three days that I drove around western Iowa in search of photographs and new alliances with artists. There have been clashes of egos, and questioning of my idiosyncratic way of choosing which artists to photograph. Since I could not find the time, money, nor energy to photograph each talented woman artist working in this state, the project could not be all inclusive. My wish that all women artists in Iowa would see this project as a celebration of their work and lives has sometimes been fulfilled and sometimes disappointed. But mostly this has been very satisfying work, involving new artistic challenges, a better sense of artistic community, a growing appreciation of my home state, and best of all, much-treasured friendships with some incredible women.

I have been both satisfied and challenged in the collaborative nature of this project, working with the artists, the designer, and the editors, as well as the writers who produced the essays that accompany the photographs. Many women have interviewed the artists, listening for life issues voiced in friendly conversation that may echo life issues faced by other artists, writers, and readers.

As my friend/writer/contributing editor Carol Lauhon has said, "Collaborative work is much like joining a marathon dance for a charitable cause. After long hours head-to-head, you think maybe you should have just given the money instead. When you finish, however, you feel a triumphant satisfaction you did not foresee when you began. Something has been achieved from within you, something that was not there before."

I am grateful to all the women who have worked with me on this project. It is a privilege to witness their dedication and talent, as together we honor the creative expression of women.

–Robbie Steinbach

1. Whitney Chadwick, *Women, Art, and Society* (London: Thames and Hudson, Ltd., 1990), p. 284.
2. C. Diane Ealy, *Creativity: A Feminine Perspective,* unpublished doctoral dissertation, the University for Humanistic Studies, San Diego, CA, 1980.

Isabel Bloom and John Bloom

Introduction

Seeing Ourselves in Each Other

Lifework shows me one woman's creative journey out of the privacy of seclusion into the public sphere. It works as a travelogue and a documentary, a journal and a memoir, a plan of action and a toast to the future. A symphony of visual languages fills my mind's ear as I turn the pages, lingering here and there, like a tourist visiting a place I thought was familiar and laughing out loud, delighted to find the ordinary feel so fresh. This vital portfolio of Iowa women artists is a gift of awareness.

When Robbie Steinbach first called to ask if I'd interview half a dozen artists in the Cedar Valley area and I agreed, I became one of many destinations on the map of her long-term project, a map which keeps unfolding blank sections of unmarked territory others would like to claim. Why didn't she photograph this artist here or that woman there? Why only women? Why only visual artists? Don't all Iowa artists deserve recognition? In phone calls we exchanged as our collaboration increased, I reminded Robbie that it was her project, her art, she could do with it as she wished.

Robbie focused her camera on the complexity of women's participation in American art and society, exploring broad generalities through individual stories. Her work multiplies the images that can come to mind when people ask the right questions—who are our artists, what are they doing, and why. These multi-faceted portraits offer a grand opening into parts of the cultural terrain shaped and experienced and imagined by women working as visual artists in Iowa over the past half century. As Carol Lauhon said, "This is a book about what women can do."

Carol Lauhon and Paddy Blackman were among the first writers affiliated with Robbie's project in the Quad Cities. I joined in 1996, and Marge Myers agreed to oversee the book's design, typesetting, and layout the following year. This past February, Robbie reserved Room C at the Iowa City Public Library for an informal afternoon meeting of the "Emulsional Support Group," the five of us involved in this book's final stages. We gathered to recall the project's history and process and to celebrate its many inspirations.

Robbie traced this book to a point in 1993 when her application for an exhibit at the Davenport Museum of Art was accepted. She had created a body of work with her "Imaging Quad Cities Women" series, but wanted word portraits to add more layers to the lifework narratives her black-and-white images implied. "I decided that I wanted text to accompany the photographs, and that I wanted the words to not be 'just the facts' as reported by me, but another kind of artwork," she said.

The smaller upstairs gallery chosen by the museum for the exhibit limited selection to two photographs of fourteen women, plus artwork by each artist. Museum staff also specified short text panels matched to the patience of readers standing in the gallery. "I explained my general idea to Vicky Morrow, a friend I walk with twice a week. I told her I wanted women who were not only gifted writers, but who would be in tune with the feminist goals of the project. She put me in touch with Carol Lauhon."

At the time, Carol led a writing workshop made up primarily of middle-aged and older women from both the Iowa and Illinois sides of the Quad Cities, known as the Now or Never Writing Class. "These talented writers had more life experience than writing experience, and they had been writing for limited audiences," Carol explained. "I thought this project would offer them a way to take their own writing seriously. This was a step toward making public their aspirations and showing them that they could be writers in public."

Writing portraits is a method of its own, just as the photographs are of a particular genre. Robbie aimed for something expected, but also something spontaneous, trying again and again and again. From the dozens of frames on several rolls of film she shot of each subject, Robbie chose only one or two images for the portrait series. "The photograph represents one moment in time and place that I have chosen," Robbie said, "but I make no claim to representing a whole person. It represents part of the truth. It's not untrue, but just a slice."

Though the writers also wish to convey a whole through partial fragments, the time exposure of a minimum two-hour interview makes a different impression that is retained for later processing. Editing images in photography and literature occurs in the moment as well as later in the studio—the strongest material selects itself out of statements, poses, moods, information both relevant and not.

For Paddy Blackman, a Now or Never class member, shaping her interviews for the show enlarged her self-image. "I had thought of myself as a writer, but I felt isolated," Paddy said. "I never realized the power that could come from collaboration. It was exciting and liberating." Working with Carol and other workshop members to polish the portraits to a spare minimum brought on discussions of identity, authenticity, and the voice of authority needed to earn readers' attention. The group also secured funding to publish their essays and Robbie's photographs in a booklet, along with additional word portraits by other area writers.

The exhibit opening had the largest attendance to date of any reception on a Sunday afternoon at the museum. "Especially for the senior members of the Now or Never class, it was a new experience for their husbands to come with them to the museum. The husbands were the active supportive partners, and for that generation at that time, it was a new thing," Carol commented. "So although we hoped to influence younger women, the creativity of this project didn't just go down through the subsequent generations, but up through the ranks, too."

The panel discussion that accompanied the first exhibit opening met with positive input and congratulations from the audience overall, but there was also a swirl of other responses. Not all of Robbie's photographs from the series were included, and some of these artist-subjects felt insulted. "This hurt and surprised me," Robbie said. "I had, perhaps naively, hoped that the artists would understand that the exhibition was limited by the museum space. The show was meant to celebrate the creativity and lives of all the women artists in the area."

Some remarks revealed the exasperating alienation and invisibility of women artists. "I mentioned to one man that my project kept growing, that I kept finding more women I wanted to photograph. He said, 'You mean there are more than three or four women artists in the Quad Cities?' A male artist and colleague questioned why the show had only women in it," Robbie said. "I felt compelled to point out to him how many shows and art history texts there have been with only men in them."

Robbie could have escorted these men downstairs to discuss the issues in the museum's larger main gallery where artworks owned by Quad Cities collectors were on display. "I think we figured that ninety to ninety-five percent of the works were by male artists," Carol recalled. The dialogue could have explored why the women's art was upstairs and the men's downstairs, or other non-art factors which influence such choices, such as economics, class, and race.

Carol had a different solution. "That very week, a tornado ripped through my cousin Mark's grocery store in rural Michigan. The tornado picked the roof up and set it down beside the store. It upturned everything inside the store. My fantasy was what if that very same tornado came by the Davenport Museum of Art, took the roof off, and just turned everything around," she said.

"The shows mixed together so you didn't know that one was from the gender ghetto and one was from the commodified art sector. They were equal, in quality, and if you took the labels off, very few could you tell would be by a woman or a man. I think that that suggests something about how we take the tag that is 'art' and we do the sorting. But actually the sorting is pretty artificial. The quality of the art or the capacity of the art to move you is not explained by the gender tag or the commercial viability of that particular artist. For the most part, these are not gender-marked works of art, but they are gender-marked lives."

Encouraged by the response to this first exhibition and partly as a result of her own interest in pursuing the theme, Robbie expanded her adventure beyond the Quad Cities. Women and their domestic labor had inspired her originally. With women artists, women and their work are united incontrovertibly. "Artists were some of the most intriguing people I knew," Robbie said. "I was 'new' as an artist, and I was probably looking for the source of creativity, and how that creativity fit into women artists' lives. I photographed colleagues, my daughter's art teacher, women I wanted to know better. Then women in the Quad Cities I didn't know personally, but whose work I admired."

More than seventy visual artists in Iowa and Illinois have "sat" for her portrait sessions. These improvisational encounters were sometimes structured, more often spur-of-the-moment, or both. When photographing a friend such as Laurie Hall, Robbie had a concept in mind. "I just knew how I wanted to make that photograph," she recalled. Some people were camera-shy. Weather was always a third party in the collaboration. Out of the whole series, she selected fifty subjects for this book. "It's a nice round number," Robbie laughed. "These fifty represent my own artistic choices."

The complete series is a trove Robbie can rearrange for different exhibitions. At a Spring 1998 show of fifteen photographs at the Muscatine Art Center, Robbie talked with a man in the gallery about his insight that the series has evolved through the most recent portraits. "He perceived the early ones as more natural, the later ones more dramatic, constructed, or manipulated. He's right," Robbie commented. He considered his analysis negative, but she appreciated it as instructive and positive. "I found I had to work harder to find new ways to think about making portraits."

Portrait writing also challenged Paddy to characterize her experience of the person without becoming journalistic or repetitive. "I didn't want to get formulaic, but a lot of the artists say the same things about their work and how they do it," Paddy said. The interview may have gone well or not, but it's all she had. After an interview, Paddy would write a draft and then listen to her tape-recording of the session where she'd often find a theme she had missed entirely. "I try to convey something that's worth knowing about them and their art. It helps to demystify art. When people tell their stories, I understand the art better."

As the years passed and subjects multiplied across Iowa, Robbie became a skilled juggler-woman-artist. Not everyone she contacted could participate. She matched out-of-town writers with artists, and used a variety of communications from e-mail to prayer, hoping that an artist whom she'd written to or called would answer after months of no reply. And once the project grew beyond the strict limitations of the Davenport exhibition, the writers could craft longer portraits, ranging from four hundred to six hundred words, about half the length of a typical newspaper or magazine feature article.

"A lot of essays begin by setting the scene—the sounds, the smells, the sense of being here at a particular moment. It put me in the frame of mind that I'm not going to get a complete story here, I just get that moment, how you saw that person presenting at that moment," Marge Myers said of typesetting the texts. "The essays paint such a graphic image of the artist, I just couldn't wait to see the photos of the artist and her work."

Since 1993, Paddy has interviewed over thirty artists for the series. She remains intrigued by the practical details of art-making as well as the ingenious ways women keep working. "One thing I never heard was, 'If I had more time.' They did their art without excuses," she said. "I've thought a lot about that Virginia Woolf ideal, 'a room of one's own.' Whether it was a physical room or a place in time they had carved out for their art, they had claimed it. And it was very definitely theirs, but they were willing to let other people in. It wasn't exclusively theirs, which I think says something about women's lives. Their lives are never exclusive. The seamlessness—cooking and then working on a print and then answering the door and then giving the kid a cookie—it's remarkable integration."

Though Carol held categories in her mind that could guide conversation from biography through technical terms during her interviews, she let the artist set boundaries and topics. "I never made any assumptions about their feminist politics. The history of their work is generally more evocative, and they usually go one way or the other—aesthetic or political. The woman artist theme was not usually part of the conversation, because they'd self-identified with the project already," Carol explained. "It makes it easy to write when you take people as they come. The subject is fully formed, not something we create from scratch. I tried to open up a life rather than take a snapshot."

Most artists approved of the finished word portraits with minor corrections, but others sent back their own versions. Some artists felt the photograph and the write-up should benefit them as marketing tools. One artist excluded herself from the book. Though no one asked to take her own photograph, some artists felt the writing was open to editorial direction. Each writer/artist pair decided the outcome. "It became an agreed-upon vision, I think, a shared vision," Paddy commented. "Any portrayal will always be incomplete and even slightly foreign to the one portrayed."

There is a deep ecology in these environmental portraits. How women use and define space, the introspective or analytical ways they approach or tamper with the boundaries of their chosen crafts and lives, the wit and wisdom they

offer willingly—these and other qualities embellish our understanding of contemporary life in the Midwest. There is no one way to be a woman artist in Iowa, but the many ways depicted here suggest an interplay between the elements woman, artist, Iowa.

The Iowa element is most obvious in the photographs—only one urban skyline out of fifty, and that's downtown Ely. The interior, exterior, and ambiguous landscapes in which we live and work act as touchstones for many of the artists in their conversations and their art. The isolation is real. The weather is constantly variable. The rivers are wide. The sky just is. "In so many photographs, there's just—space," Paddy said, shaking her head, scanning for a better term. "Just—space. Tons of space."

Rather than travel to the Twin Cities or New York or Chicago to photograph possibly more famous artists, Robbie chose to find meaning at home. She started with the women she knew, and the circle of friends grew wider as each contact gave new recommendations and suggestions. If silence is a preferred social norm in the Midwest, as some people argue, then that's another boundary crossed by the women in this book. Their conversational intimacy relaxes the tensions between life and work, community and family, artist and audience.

"What is an artist? I considered myself an artist since age ten. After reading several of these texts, I began to question whether or not I belong to that group," Marge reflected. "There is such a sense of suffering, of struggling, such eccentric lives. They've worked so hard on their personas, and have used their art to deal with so much personal growth or in finding their identity."

"Many of the artists have lived long enough to have had tragic experiences, life sufferings that aren't directly connected to their art," Paddy added. "If anything, this makes a case for an expanded definition of artist, like Alice Walker says of her mother in *In Search of Our Mothers' Gardens.*"

The book also makes the case for an expanded discussion of women's participation in society—whether as Iowans, women, or artists. "Our common understanding is that boys in our culture seem to grow up with a sense of entitlement, so that if they want to do art, they are entitled to do it, and they are entitled to receive cultural, familial support for doing it," Carol said. "This has been the pattern until, say, the 1970s, for women to feel inspiration, but not necessarily to feel entitlement. To be creative, but under the wing of the house, at home. And not to, for example, spend the family nest egg on a kiln or a studio, or in other words, to do it with your left hand because your right hand is for whatever—marriage, children, domestic responsibilities, or wage-earning that is predictable rather than risky."

Echoes of these limitations surface in many of the artists' interviews, whether they had or have children or husbands or partners or not. And yet, these women act. "What's been interesting to me about visiting with these artists is that they will talk about inspiration, generally speaking, they will talk about how they got into art, but you never hear a discrete moment of entitlement," Carol recalled. "It must have happened, but there's a

certain modesty about saying, 'This is me. I'm putting it all on the table. I'm putting it all at risk.' I think they lived it, but I never heard that expressed."

"We hear in women's studies that women don't talk about their accomplishments because that's seen as bragging, and bragging is something that women aren't supposed to do but men are allowed to do," Robbie said. "And we're also taught that we should be nurturing and self-sacrificing, which aren't necessarily bad things, but if that's all we can be, then it's very selfish for us to do something for ourselves—which art has to be, since art comes from the self."

The synergy between many of the portraits is a part of Robbie's project she did not control or create, but which adds an intangible and welcome aspect. Most of the photographs and the writers' interviews were taken separately, sometimes months or years apart. Most of the writers didn't see Robbie's photographs until long after their word portraits were completed. "There's certainly something about Naomi," Carol said of the visual and word portraits of Naomi Schedl. "The harmony is stunning. There's some kind of external validation, an external meaning that is bigger than all of us."

Looking at the completed works of a decade-long series involving dozens of collaborators, Robbie feels gratified that "it all fits together." "One thing I gained from this work was a greater sense of being an artist in a community of artists. We're so spread out in this state, as opposed to being all in one city or an area of a city, and because of the popular perception that there aren't many of us, it was important to me to confirm that there is this incredible community of artists working in Iowa. I got to know a lot of artists and they got to know me, but another good thing that happened is that they got to know each other," she commented.

"Sometimes I think about what author Sandra Cisneros once said at a conference I attended in her home city of San Antonio, Texas, about her time at the Iowa Writers' Workshop in Iowa City. She said, 'What I learned about working in Iowa was to make art as if no one would ever see it.' While of course that isn't entirely true—all of these artists have shown their art extensively in Iowa and elsewhere—one thing that struck me was how each artist perseveres in her art, despite the fact that some of her neighbors may not understand or appreciate it, that her work may never be seen in the 'big' markets of New York or LA, that Iowa has some of the lowest public funding for the arts. They just keep making art for the satisfaction and life-enhancing 'hell and joy' of it."

These portraits don't show the beginnings, middles, or ends of women's stories, but they do assure us of complexity. We appreciate the varieties of women we are. We listen to the women we know. We find the women we want to meet. We touch the women we strive to become. We see each other as strong and vulnerable people who claim awe and joy, sadness and intelligence, doubt and wonder. These portraits encourage us to talk seriously

with one another, to play, to examine and explore our surroundings, and to risk feeling at ease in the presence of strangers.

The possibilities for women artists in Iowa shimmer in the linked vocabularies. The art words of tong, burin, warp, contour, glory hole, press, easel, raku, chalk, canvas, keystroke, charcoal, glop, emulsion, press, slip, digital imaging, needle, dye, sketch, loom. Purple, black, chocolate, azure, yellow, red, gold, green, indigo, white. The domestic rags, casseroles, irons, nightgowns, cornstarch, dough, skillets, slip, soup, cookies, batiste. The landscape of memory, passion, ritual, love, dream, future, exploration, laughter. The world of reed, corn, night, river, gorge, field, willow, nest, tornado, space, seaweed, bone, snails, sticks, antlers, sky. The social realm of death, doorway, newsprint, citizen, workbench, audience, risk, protest, identity, wisdom, home, family. The spirit energy, alive, ancient, magic, connected, happy, devotional, light, protective, indestructible, primordial, female.

Marianne Abel

Pam Dennis

Pam Dennis stokes her outdoor wood-burning kiln late into the night. She notices a few cars driving by slowly on the usually empty gravel road. "Probably curious neighbors," she speculates. Pam acknowledges that she and her family are a curiosity in their small farming community.

A purple mailbox marks the driveway into the landscape of converted farm buildings, animals, and a tangled plush collection of vegetable and flower gardens. This is a rich world for artists. Pam first explored art with her paternal aunt, a talented actress, who encouraged Pam to become an artist in her teens. Her aunt remained a staunch supporter until her death five years ago.

In Dennis' compound, family roots stretch everywhere, including the gathering place in the kitchen. Friends and family pull up chairs around the yellow formica table, inherited from her grandparents. Lean back and swap stories. This is a family of storytellers. She has an anecdote for everything around her, from the arched iron yard gate built as a monument to a favorite dog to the beachball-size ceramic spheres nestled in the gardens. The pottery globes, glazed in a palette of hues and metallic finishes, are works she rejected. "If they crack during firing, or if I am not satisfied with the end result, I find a place for them in the yard."

The yard, centered by the kiln, is circled by buildings. The gray barn houses the sophisticated sound equipment of her musician husband. Her studio is a low red wooden shed. Waist-high tables line the walls of her workspace. Evidence of her productivity covers the tabletops—clay work in a variety of stages, bunches of collected willow reeds, jars, books, and copper circles. A white cast mold of a woman's torso, used in an installation piece, lies eerily on a table. A cat jumps up and walks gingerly among the collections. Pam scoops him up and cradles him in her arms, stroking his furry back as she recounts projects and pieces recently completed.

As an artist working in various media she is involved in many art venues—shows, galleries, school and community workshops, and fairs. One room in her house is devoted to finished work. It is stacked with willow tripod stands for ceramic globes, wall hangings of wood, weavings incorporating found objects, metal, and clay.

"I have always had an urge to learn new things," Pam reflects. This urge led her to Nicaragua the past two summers where she worked as a potter and teacher. She recorded the project on video and photographed local people.

Pam sits at the kitchen table, answering a community art request. She intends to propose something different, a way to continue her exploration of the world of art.

෨ *Paddy Blackman*

Verna Banks-Craighead

She was a legal secretary then a homemaker. "My impulse to do art came late. I had no idea I had any talent."

When her childcare responsibilities ended, Verna enrolled with a neighbor in an evening class in the Davenport Community School District. "My first attempt looked like it could be rather nice work," she smiles, "so once I started I never stopped!" Thereafter she took classes at the Davenport Museum of Art and other master workshops, studied art history, attended lectures and exhibitions, and joined Studio 15 Gallery.

Verna began traveling around the country to workshops and exhibitions a decade ago. "On the plane to Reno for my first workshop, I discovered Barbara Nechis, the instructor for the course. I took a deep breath and introduced myself. We shared a nice conversation and, later at the airport, the services of a redcap. We had a wonderful workshop, and we still correspond."

Verna stays in touch with artists everywhere. She invokes each name precisely, recalling with feeling where and when she first worked with them, and what they're doing now. At her fingertips is the membership book for the Women's Caucus for the Arts. Tucked inside the Caucus book is a list headed "Coast-to-Coast Women of Color." Her name is on both lists. She acts with others in support of women's art.

At the very first national caucus she attended, Verna was nominated from the floor for a seat on the board. Her term lasted three years. She serves currently as Midwestern Region Vice President. "I've made wonderful friends through the caucus."

Verna first became known as a watercolorist. Now she works with printmaking, handmade paper, ink drawings, and oil crayon as well. Her studio work at home is rich with experiences of the world she has drawn into her life.

ᔈ Carol Lauhon

Marcia Wegman

She lives in a shingled cottage by the side of the road. Tucked against a bluff near the Iowa River and filled with natural light, the storybook house is painted a warm dark brown. And trimmed in gentian violet.

Marcia Wegman celebrates the unexpected, the unknown, the paradoxical. In a room filled with antiques, an array of whitened animal bones adorns a shelf like so many porcelain figurines. She is a passionate gardener whose favorite pastime is reading, an artist schooled in printmaking who explores many media.

"Double Landscape, Winter and Spring" graces one wall of the cottage. The two abstracts are a print-collage of waxed paper, pasteled shapes, penciled lines, and handmade paper. But the companion pieces offer much more than pastel colors and soft paper, so easy on the eye. Angular lines strengthen the work, and a metallic aura energizes them. Their rain-washed colors vibrate with an underlying tension, just as the promise of spring holds the unease of change.

"It's transitions like that from winter to spring that I find so exciting. The doing of art is mystical. Artists try to represent what we know—nature close-up—as well as what's hidden and unknowable."

Marcia's own journey toward the unknowable has transported her from printmaking to paper jewelry to acrylic landscapes to paint and pastel still-lifes. Painted from close-up photographs, her recent work depicts flowers large and lush and sensual. "Exquisite microcosms," she says. "In graduate school, working from photographs was considered beneath

a 'real' artist, and watercolors were only for Sunday painters." But then in graduate school, women students weren't regarded as serious artists.

Marcia continued her work even after her children were born. But one day, when her son began drawing on her canvas, she packed away her artist's tools and shifted her focus to other endeavors. She raised her children and ran a local shop filled with an eclectic mix of treasures, "and for fifteen years, did no art at all."

When she unleashed her gift again, her work was more mature, professional, refined, experimental, creative. Work enlivened by her experience and inspired by nature and a profound spirituality.

Losing a father when you are nine and a son when he is twelve will do that to you.

Marcia has always been searching for something. As a child, she loved caves. Their cool embrace seemed at once ancient and familiar. She uses the same words to describe death.

"I have, perhaps, a different perspective on death. It is such an important part of nature, and that has a direct relationship with my art. I think we have memories of our pre-birth lives, and we remain with those who love us. The knowledge of this enriches our current life and work."

She looks through several of her recent paintings, exotic flowers from close-up and landscapes from a distance. A splash of deep turquoise swells the petals of a Mexican blossom, and a spectral blue whispers across a Western sky. Marcia clearly revels in all the contrasts of her life—printmaking and painting, abstraction and hyper-realism, flowers and bones.

❧ *Jean Florman*

Robbie Steinbach

In an early self-portrait, she stands in a nightgown at the ironing board. "With this series I could say: housework is real work. I made the invisible visible." The iron is poised above the board. Stuffed wildlife, evidence of her stepfather's hobby, inhabits the walls around her.

"There was a stasis in that portrait. I wasn't an English teacher anymore. I wasn't working at the F-Stop anymore. My daughter would be starting school. Freelance work wasn't allowing me to say what I wanted to say."

Mirrors began appearing in her self-portraits. "I was trying to get a look at myself." Imaging other women, women with children, was important to her too. She began photographing professionals juggling multiple roles. "I wanted to know how they did it."

Photographic study at the University of Iowa and teaching photography at Augustana College in the same year led to a coalescence: "Photography was the lifework I'd been looking for."

She continued exploring self-portraiture. In "The Works" from her "Wise Woman" series, Robbie stands facing the viewer, smiling slightly. Her right hand clasps a mirror and a baby doll. Her left hand holds the book, *Woman's Body: An Owner's Manual*. At her feet are a plunger, a Barbie doll in bridal garb, and a fur stole nestled around household cleaners and a coffee mug. Around her neck she has slung her own camera.

Her camera has also provided alternatives to conventional images of beauty. Such conventional images linger as shadows in women's quests to see themselves. So says Robbie's "Marilyn and Me" series, for which she carried around a life-sized cardboard icon of Marilyn Monroe for a day. In one self-portrait, Robbie applies make-up, Marilyn looks on, and the mirror reflects them both. Between the images is a shadow—Robbie's own—and she has cast it herself.

‿ *Carol Lauhon*

Clary Illian

The past is part of every pot Clary Illian throws. Motioning to rows of unfired covered dishes and footed bowls lining her studio, she says, "My pots express the history of pottery." Her dedication to ceramic traditions began in Cornwall, England, during a two-year apprenticeship under Bernard Leach, renowned potter, historian, and a lifelong student of Japanese folk pottery.

A professional, Clary produces utilitarian ceramic pieces in large quantities. Her business card offers stoneware and porcelain "safe for oven, microwave, and dishwasher." She wants her work used as well as admired. "I intend to make the best pot I can, but utility sets the parameters."

"I interpret forms rather than creating them," says Clary, who signs her work with a small stamp, her initials recreating a pot in the abstract. The stamp is a reluctant nod to the marketplace. She prefers anonymity. Her craft has supported her since the mid-1960's when she set up her first studio in rural Benton County.

Clary lives and works simply and independently in a gray two-story building on Main Street in Ely. She built two high-temperature kilns in the backyard to fire her prolific production, and sells her work exclusively from the storefront shop, marketing by word of mouth and two yearly mailings.

Today there are no apprenticeships available for beginning ceramists. Clary offers guidance to young potters but dreams of more—of securing the funding to develop apprenticeships in her own studio, of infusing the present with the past, of passing to others the long traditions.

ॐ Paddy Blackman

Karin Stevens Connelly

Karin Stevens Connelly's art offers a closet full of memories. In her work you can see an old friend, the consequences of war, the threat of homelessness, the quirks and stereotypes of family and society.

Karin hoards. "We all have this problem. If you threw away everything as soon as you're done with it, you wouldn't have anything left." That's what closets are for.

Karin brings stuff out of the closets—hers, yours, the neighbor's, the world's—and uses them to articulate ideas in installations. Sculpture. Paintings. Bookmaking. Knitting. Papermaking. Karin has a certain do-it-your-own-way style. Metal wire sculpture. A Daniel Day Lewis-esque self-portrait painted on the back of a *The Last of the Mohicans* movie poster. Beadwork, memorializing her mother, made while apprenticing with Meskwaki beadworkers. "I learned how to be with someone who was patient and enduring and not uncritical, but whose criticism you had to ask for."

A 65-foot sculpture called "The River/The Waste Stream" made with Naomi Schedl, one of her professors at the University of Iowa. Juxtaposed ideas. Contrasts between toxicity in beauty and beauty in toxicity.

In college, she studied English, but always took art courses. "To me, art and life are inseparable." Karin made shirts out of paper for a while. These are not sportswear-inspired shirts you could wear on the street or out to lunch. You look at them. Maybe hang them on your wall. Definitely not in your closet. They were popular. People liked them. She stopped making them. "I do not want to spend my life making shirts even if people like them and they're made out of paper. I didn't leave these behind, I just went somewhere else."

Karin prefers collaborative art. "I get tired of my own ideas." Her favorite project was a site-specific installation that she constructed with the prisoners at the Iowa Security Medical Facility. "It was a terrifying and exhilarating experience. You had to count the pliers every few minutes. But you know, I realized that I got along as well with these people who were making art as I did with other middle-class housewives like myself."

Scrounging for materials is not uncommon for Karin. She asks friends and neighbors to save their fortune cookie fortunes and dryer lint for her. "It really strikes you how much stuff passes through your hands everyday. Stuff you always see, everyday, and you don't recognize." Karin does. When her mother was dying, Karin spent three weeks with her and her father. Talking. Doing laundry. She saved the dryer lint. Now it's part of an installation, along with photographs of her mother as she was dying.

Karin is willing to be in your face. If she thinks it's important. Make you rethink your beliefs. Ideologies come through in paintings like, "Things the Surgeon General Can't Say." She tries out her ideas at the Sit 'n Knit. She tries her ideas out on anyone she can. "I want my work to be as clear as possible, but I also don't want it to be offensive because then people will turn away from it."

And when it's time to start a new project, Karin returns to the closet. "Stuff makes your life and gets in the way of your life, but it also shapes your life and helps you remember your life."

It's all about where you've been and where you've got to go.

∽ *Denise Lamphier*

Kristin Quinn

Life flows in the earthen tones of Kristin Quinn's creations. "Oil paint," she says, "is the most life-like substance."

She paints in layers without many clues. "I do not have a plan to guide the work. I start instead by accumulating things, piling them one on top of the other. Forms are buried, hidden, composed and decomposed countless times."

The painting may become difficult to navigate. "Then I find a foothold. Color will most often serve this need. Associating an indigo and Indian yellow mixture might, for example, lead to the texture and form of wet seaweed. A warm yellow-gray might trigger a strange metallic shape." Kristin prefers to paint with the canvas in her lap. She surrounds herself and you with the work. What motivates her: form, tension, aggression, and obsession.

"I have to let the painting evolve. Yet it takes a lot of force and aggression to get the images out. I work meandering spirals into crescendo."

By placing and superimposing images she brings the forms to fruition. The painting is developed in layers like skin on a body, or strata of earth. "Form and uniform, fragile and massive, growth and decay, organic and geometric, those tensions give the painting force. Its outer form occurs when all parts have been fully developed and are bound together. All irreconcilable differences are synthesized."

Kristin's obsession with art spans her lifetime. Even if she were the only observer of her work, she would continue. Nevertheless, "You make art because you want to affect people."

꙰ Teresa Ruzic

Shirley Wyrick

Shirley Wyrick's images evolve, floating and whittled in time in her mind. Her challenge is to bring the work of her imagination into a physical world where she cuts, melts, and welds. In the process of production, Shirley's images develop toward their final translation into metal. Recently she bolted points of a sculpture to the sides of lucite towers so that her piece would appear suspended, as suspended as it appeared to her when still just an image in her mind.

A friend has described Shirley as a "lateral thinker" who includes the community in her creation of art. She has borrowed from the expertise of everyone from auto body shop specialists to geologists. She strives "to think outside the usual lines," stretching toward new connections, expanding conventional limits, exploring diverse creative paths. She may work with ladders or trees, fires, paths or rivers.

Her three-story work "The River: Time Is A River Without Banks" was installed in the Johnson County Administration Building. The installation celebrates the Iowa River. Cast metals appear to flow down the building's interior. "Iowa's lifeblood is its rivers," says Shirley, "but rivers have shifting boundaries. When lines change, so does meaning."

Shirley must maintain physical strength and stamina. The cast steel and iron sculptures are huge. The months from proposal to installation are long. She maintains creative flexibility and fluency by drawing with charcoal, an activity she calls "art aerobics."

The artist's home serves as a retrospective gallery of her work. Three sculptures stand on pedestals in the living room, and two layered needle-drawings, made with an unthreaded sewing machine, hang on a wall opposite two charcoal "aerobics." The lower level houses Shirley's five-room studio where she has the space and equipment her work requires. A large-windowed room where she makes wax and plastilene patterns is bright with winter sunlight. Outside, snow covers the winding hosta garden. On a slight rise to the right, anchored in the earth, stands a ten-foot-high sculpture in the form of a primordial projectile erected by the artist-in-residence.

Shirley continues to affirm her fierce belief in community art, a belief that led her to the presidency of ARTS IOWA CITY. Under her leadership, the center was renovated and expanded. Even as she continues to provide bridges between individual artists and the community, however, Shirley finds herself shifting more time back to the world of her own imagination, an interior world which challenges her to translate its images into art the rest of us may share.

ᔕ *Paddy Blackman*

Mary E. Young Bear

Mary Young Bear is a thirty-eight-year-old single parent who lives with her four children on the Meskwaki Settlement near Tama. "I stay at home with my kids because casino money affords me that luxury." She is proud of her cultural traditions. She also believes in diversity, partially as a result of growing up in Denver, Colorado. There she learned to enjoy the symphony and museums and galleries.

"I've always been a square peg around here," she laughs. "I try to expose my kids to different kinds of art, artists, work from different periods. I think it's starting to make a difference." She can sew or draw quietly at night while her kids fall asleep to classical music.

When she was eight, her grandmother gave her a "starter kit" for beading, and she remembers being inspired by the dancers' costumes at a pow-wow she attended with her father. Growing up poor taught her, too. She was the oldest daughter among five children that her mother abandoned, and her father turned to her to help raise her siblings. "That's how I learned how to sew. I had no choice."

Now she creates elaborately beaded costumes for her sons and daughters and other family members, and smaller-scale items fitted to handsewn dolls. Many of her functional garments start as individual pieces, such as arm bands, leggings, barrettes, yokes, and sashes. Each item is beaded with a variation on a color and pattern scheme that becomes a vibrant display when the matched outfit is worn together. She blends her knowledge of Meskwaki and Plains Indians patterns with her own flair for symmetrical floral and abstract motifs in brilliant colors. "I always try to think of something original, something different."

She initially sought nursing training at Marshalltown Community College, but while touring the campus, an art professor convinced her to take a drawing class. At Marshalltown and later at Coe College, she found her vocation in printmaking. "Beadwork is more tactile and visual. With printmaking, the work I do is real spontaneous and more emotional," Mary explains. "When I'm making prints, I have no sense of time. I used to be that way about beadwork; it never felt like work. Now if I could just do printmaking, I'd do it all the time.

"When I was really little, I used to have the same recurring dream, from when I was three or four until I was twelve or thirteen years old." Mary could anticipate when the dream would come, and usually she looked forward to it. In the dream, she is a large rock and other stones are present. "They have a way of communicating. In my culture, we treat stones and all aspects of nature with the same respect we show our elders. My dad said maybe that's why I'm drawn to printmaking. That's what I was put in this world to do, to work with those stones. I would like to be known as a printmaker."

ᕍ Marianne Abel

Connie Bieber

Connie Bieber paints and lives in a square yellow house on a busy city road. But behind the house it seems like the country, with two weathered red barns, a garden, and a pasture where her flock of sheep rest.

"Sometimes I happen on stunning moments of quiet beauty as I care for my sheep. It might be in the way the sheep are standing or in the way the light hits the wool." The pastoral life provides Connie moments of relief and inspiration in her full schedule.

Working in watercolor, Bieber uses the world in her eye as an entry into the surreal. The surprises occur in the placement of images. "Dance of the Seasons" portrays a stand of trees, each in a different season. Snow on a bare branch laps over a limb in full green leaf. In "Fearless Flying," a small female figure flies in space, holding on to the tendril of a giant fuschia flower. The juxtaposition of images creates layers of meaning.

"I like to layer my colors, too," Connie says as she discusses the deep intensity of hues.

An oval female face with blue eyes framed by pale strawberry blond hair describes both the artist and the female figure in her work.

This persona looks back at you in "The Paradise of a Garden," and is draped as a classic statue in "Reliquary Alignment." Her work questions family, intimacy, and spiritual energy.

Connie has supported herself and her son with her art for over a dozen years. Numerous galleries carry her work. She regularly prints hundreds of a finished commercial piece.

The sun slants through the uncurtained window onto Connie's drafting table. Flute music soothes the air. She can look up and gaze out at the barns and pasture. The table is scattered with books, calendars, brochures. She pencils images, rearranging the various elements until an idea crystallizes. Satisfied with the composition, Connie begins to paint, meticulously, mixing colors in a six-cup muffin tin. After awhile, she'll put down her brush and go out to the barn, pick a few weeds in the garden, "nurturing the muse" with everyday chores.

Paddy Blackman

Colleen Ernst

olleen Ernst will never forget her first attempt to land a professional position. Fresh from an undergraduate education in art history at Northwestern University, Colleen approached the Art Institute of Chicago about the possibility of working there. "They told me, 'We don't have any jobs for you in art history, but you can apply to our cafeteria if you like.'"

As she is wont to do, Colleen laughed. Then she turned her sights elsewhere, working as a secretary at Northwestern, an English teacher in Japan, and eventually as an art teacher in the public schools. And a professional artist.

Colleen says that as a young woman, she pursued art history because she didn't consider herself an artist. Yet today her distinctive energetic work is widely admired. And when Colleen first began teaching art to local elementary school children, she told herself, "OK, I'd better start finding out what I'm doing." Twenty years later, she is beloved by a generation of children whose fledgling artistic efforts she nurtured and refined.

Colleen's basement studio reflects her many artistic personae. A few years ago, the Iowa City artist was intrigued with the idea of incorporating found objects, like skulls or an old saxophone or the suit her husband Bill wore on their wedding day, into large sculptural assemblages. She paved the surfaces with other found objects: scraps of velvet, garish costume jewelry, plastic "Little People," tiny teacups. The pieces were frenetic, exuberant, and eye-catching.

"But I got tired of preservation. The glue wouldn't hold, and people would bump into the sculptures, and protecting them under Plexiglas was just too expensive. It was time for a change."

So Colleen decided to focus on color instead. "It was very gratifying to find my work flattening out, dealing with paint and canvas. There's just a pureness about color, a directness. It's just a lot more 'down to it.'"

The "down to it" applies to the process of painting, too. But there are so many distractions. The washing machine is just over there next to the studio. And time for creative work must be carved out of evenings, weekends, and summers. Colleen adds that she needs solitude to paint—solitude and really loud music. Van Morrison works. "I crank it way up and jump around the studio. The kids complain it's too loud."

As she rubs her hands over the acrylic pinks, blues, and whites embracing the image of a lime green Mexican pot, Colleen adds that creating a painted image on blank canvas is very different from the additive process of creating sculptures from found objects.

"I think these paintings are more fluid, less cluttered, and easier on the eye than my earlier sculptures. Before, I'd see an object and try to transform it by applying another object. Now as I paint, I suddenly discover an image or arrive at a whole work that I never knew existed before. Somehow things just emerge, and I'm not always even sure what they represent. But the images are transcendent. For me, the best state to be in is when I forget everything else and am consumed by color and shape."

& *Jean Florman*

Carol Macomber

Carol Macomber processes film in a cramped alley of the basement of her house in Cedar Falls. The smaller and darker the space, the better. But developing film is only part of her artistic process. In another corner, she sets up lights and fabrics to create just the scenario she wants for staging her still lifes. She has shot some of her favorite work upstairs by placing objects on a wooden bench below a window in the living room. Actually, her real studio is elsewhere. Carol's primary subject is nature.

She brings the outside in and turns the inside out for closer study. She wants her photographs to speak about aspects of nature that don't have a voice so their quiet presence stays alive in the public imagination. "There's less and less space for creatures other than ourselves. We're not leaving much room." One series depicts amphibians and reptiles stored in glass jars at the University Museum. Carol wants to document the animals of Black Hawk County—the specimens in museum drawers. If it's in the county, she considers it part of our environment.

Carol approaches photography with a creative blend of technical and scientific skills that extend beyond her college training in biology and her initial employment in a surgical research laboratory. Raised in upstate New York, she learned that life was work. "Anything fun wasn't work." She never considered art a serious endeavor until she moved to Iowa over twenty years ago, after eight years in foreign countries. She became intrigued with large format, black-and-white photography when she lived in Ankara and saw an Edward Weston exhibition.

"One thing that really pleases me is to give plants and animals the portraiture lighting that we give to people." Arranging bones and antlers or shells and plants is her version of playing with dolls, something she never did as a child. "I'm just as simple-minded as ever," she laughs. "The bigger the camera, the more seriously I take it." She aims her 4" x 5" at the big picture that worries her most, the destruction of habitat and environmental diversity.

Carol knows that we look at photographed objects as if they were real. "I think of art as a philosophy, something that helps us think about things." She hopes her work shows us what we might not see or in ways we might not choose on our own, but she never wanted to be a teacher. "I don't like to say things more than once. That's why pictures are good. Look again if you want."

For a current series of photograms of prairie grasses, she adapted an antique cyanotype process to join her respect for the past and her experience of the present with a message for the future. She coats six-foot sheets of watercolor paper with iron salts, lays down a plant specimen under a sheet of glass, and exposes the assemblage to sunlight. The final print registers a troubling image.

The green salt wash mixed with half an hour of Iowa sunshine turns the blue hue of that time, and the prairie grass becomes a highly detailed ghost. "Such grasses once stood in groups covering thirty million acres of Iowa land and gradually over thousands of years produced the rich soil of Iowa," she comments. "It is time to reflect on our disquieting relationship with the natural world."

꙰ *Marianne Abel*

Concetta Morales

Concetta Morales moves her hands down over the contour of her rounded belly, her second child close to birth. Pregnancy has inspired her to create a series of forty-four oil stick paintings exploring peppers, a fruit as round and taut as she is.

"I hardly ever work in a series," Concetta says, acknowledging that the changes in her body announce to others the changes in her life.

The artist's studio, however, has not changed. Concetta has worked on the fourth floor of a converted warehouse in downtown Des Moines for the last ten years. The studio walls are alive with slashes and bursts of lush colors, making the huge space organic, a jungle of color against a white background. To work, she tapes paper to the wall. Her strokes are generous and often fly off the page. Each finished piece leaves behind an empty rectangle of color. The wall is a work of its own, a mural of increasingly complex design created by the outlines of rectangles.

"I will have to paint the wall white again when I can't find a clean space." She will need to paint soon, I think, at least above the waist. Below waist level, the wall is clean white except for a ten-foot stretch topped with butcher paper dense with drawings. "Remnants of my son's second birthday party. I had ten children here."

Children have always gathered and worked in Morales' studio. It's the kind of place kids love—a big worktable, a couch, a boom box, shelves of supplies, and an indestructible cement floor. Children from Cedar Rapids shelters came here to design and construct a mosaic mural for their municipal airport. Concetta estimates that she has fifty such community art murals dotting the Midwest. A group of at-risk youth in Chicago called their mural "Positive Moves in the Game of Life," depicting a human face confronting a string of obstacles.

Concetta became interested in mosaic through studying Islamic art. A friend led her to Morocco where she filled sketchbooks with the mosaics of the mosques. The mosaic technique is well-suited to community art. Pieces from discarded tiles or glass, or stones and pebbles gathered from the ground, can serve the design. Participants love the process as much as they admire their completed work.

Two large vivid paintings hang high above the workspace of Morales' studio. They face each other so viewers bend their heads back and pivot 180 degrees, looking from one to the other. In each, the figure of a baby centers the abstract collection of bright colors. "I am thinking about this side of heaven," Concetta laughs as she looks up at the works, "but also supply on demand, nursing a baby."

Concetta Morales is documenting her personal journey through motherhood in her art. And she continues to mother countless children in the creation of their own art.

꙰ *Paddy Blackman*

Jane Gilmor

Walking a dusty road in Greece, Jane Gilmor knelt down to examine a roadside shrine, drawn by the color and design, curious about the meaning. Since that day, she has trekked several continents documenting and studying roadside art. Shrines and grottos are shelter, made from things at hand, and housing candles, food, relics, and religious items. Jane calls them "homes for the soul." They are the work of untrained artists, people compelled to express and explore events in their lives. Jane has found that the meaning of these shrines is reflected in her own art.

"I love things that are simultaneously precious and mundane." She is drawn to folk art because it bridges the physical and spiritual planes of existence, and demonstrates the human impulse to create myth and art from our personal stories.

Her own art, combining metal repoussé with video, film, and photo documentation, has grown progressively larger. Current works require whole rooms for installation. The viewer walks around and then into "WINDOWS", an eight-by-eight-by-five-foot house constructed of wood and covered with the etched metal drawings and writings by pediatric patients and their families from the University of Iowa Hospitals and Clinics. Inside, a video of the child artists plays continuously as viewers study the panels. The collection creates a devotional space.

Gilmor uses objects that society has forgotten. Her thirty-foot-long windowed studio in the CSPS Art Center in Cedar Rapids is a repository of twenty years of collecting, everything from a department store mannequin to notes found on the sidewalk. "As my studio grew larger so did my work," Jane grins, brushing back her curled hair and revealing the votive leg earring. A cat's face dangles from her other ear.

Found objects and lost people. Jane recently completed a series of projects with homeless people in Midwest shelters. The process and the product of Gilmor's art reveal her willingness to face a complex and contrasting world. Jane explores the silly and the sad, the discarded and the sublime.

ᔐ *Paddy Blackman*

Louise Kames, BVM

Louise Kames studies the Mississippi River every morning, observing the point of the horizon where the sun rises, noting how the colors and light change each day as the sun shifts. In winter she conducts her morning ritual from a window in the fifth story of the motherhouse of the Mt. Carmel Convent. In the summer she goes out on the porch off the apartment she shares with five other nuns. She lives with over a hundred Sisters of Charity. She reveals the community collection of earnings, the requests she must make for things like a car.

Her days begin with watchful serenity at the convent, but move to noisy activity at Clarke College where Louise is an associate professor. She teaches four classes a semester, varying her subjects from printmaking to digital imaging and color theory. Her office is cluttered with books, file cabinets, framed prints, art supplies, and easy chairs. Her work space contrasts with the orderliness of her sparse living quarters. But her office, too, is up high, on the top floor, with a balcony that offers a wide view of campus.

Her treetop vistas are reflected in an installation piece featuring seven bird feeders suspended in front of seven framed prints. The bird feeders, archetypally house-shaped, have transparent fronts revealing reliquary objects she remembers from her paternal grandmother's home—roots, buttons, apple peels, zinnia buds, shavings of Dove soap, surgical gloves, and a feather. Each monoprint comments on the contents of the accompanying bird feeder. This is the first of her "Grandmother Pieces."

"Elegy for Ellen" is another, an installation of four wooden ironing boards, suspended on a wall and gilded. In front of each hangs a gossamer panel of batiste, the fabric of baptisms and wedding garments. An etching of gladioli is printed on the batiste, another includes a letter from her grandmother.

In a large studio filled with natural light, Kames works on "Coming Home," a print of a spiral nest, entwined and tornadic, overlain with another one of her grandmother's letters and a woman's undershirt. "I am interested in exploring vulnerability, the dynamics of personal grief in a public space."

Louise lives and works in community but her art explores an individual view of the meaning of the ordinary and their elevation towards the divine.

ﾟ *Paddy Blackman*

Jean Berry

Jean Berry is gathering pieces of her heart to create a collage, the story of granddaughter Averi's first three years of life. No doubt the collage will be huge, because Jean "can't work small." Averi will be drawn in charcoal, as Jean works from photos. The emotions of Averi's life will be captured by Berry's firm lines and softened forms. If Berry stays true to her earlier drawings, Averi's hands and eyes will be prominent features in the collage. "Eyes are the window to the soul, and hands are the sum of the experience of life," she says.

For more than twelve years, Jean has been creating charcoal drawings. She's explored new media and new techniques, finding ways to express joy and sorrow, life and growth and happiness, her own and others'.

While she willingly includes new media in her finished pieces, she loves charcoal drawings, and incorporates them into nearly all of her works. "I like the black and white drawings, because you're not distracted from the emotion in the drawing," Berry says.

One of her newest works is a self-image sculpture, "Position of Three," that depicts puberty, maturity, and old age. "I'm 'maturity' now! I've lived through puberty, and I used my imagination to create the 'old age,'" she says with a laugh.

The large sculpture is a combination of media and Jean's experiences. Draping burlap, she created three torsos. Each torso features a doll, which Berry made, and she has embellished the torsos with fabric, copper sheets and copper wire, plus charcoal drawings, acrylic paint, and oil stick.

The sculpture is anchored by three skillets in a pile of sand. Puberty is represented by the new skillet, maturity by a well-used one, and old age by a burned, damaged skillet.

"I'm not sure how viewers will interpret the skillets, or whether women will like the idea of the stages of their lives being represented by skillets," she says.

Berry enjoys the ardent support of her family—husband Lee, son S. Torriano Berry, an independent film maker, and daughter Venise Berry, a writer and associate professor of journalism.

"My children are my best critics. At some point, they decided they didn't need a mother anymore, but they wanted an artist. So now I've become the artist they can promote, and they have done so very successfully."

Berry's third child, her youngest daughter, also profoundly affected her art. Toni died of cancer at nineteen.

"I was motivated by Toni's death, and the encouragement of Chaney Rosenbaum, a Des Moines area artist with whom I had studied for about sixteen years. Chaney suggested it was time to go back to school. I had to find something to fill the void, and my art was an avenue for me to express these inner feelings. I geared myself up to develop my talent and be the best that I can be. Toni will always be a special part of my soul."

Today granddaughter Averi, who Berry calls "my heart," is never far from her thoughts.

"I make art for myself, but I'm doing something for Averi, too. At the University of Iowa's request, I'm leaving my papers to the Iowa Women's Archives. I thought it was strange that they would want my papers, but a friend said, 'Don't do it for yourself, do it for your granddaughter.' So I am," Jean says.

❧ Dawn Bowman

Martha Yoder

A fire burns in the black iron stove in the corner of the dining room. Martha Yoder offers homemade bread. The uncurtained windows frame the gray day and a landscape of now bare trees, each planted by the printmaker and her husband, Darvin. The white square farmhouse shares the yard with two barns and fenced pens. Beyond is the pasture where eighty ewes in thick wooly coats are grazing. The ewes are business, sold for the spring market.

Martha Yoder grew up in the west, moved to the plains for college, and intended to continue her journey eastward to New York City for graduate work, but fate intervened. A student she had met briefly in Kansas at her Mennonite college was teaching in Laos in lieu of military service during the Vietnam War. He wrote and asked her to join him. Her mother urged her to accept his offer, considering Laos much safer than New York City. Martha rejected the art school scholarship, and married the teacher and fellow artist the day after she arrived in Laos.

The spirit of exploration fuels Yoder. She journeyed to a Mennonite camp for delinquent boys where she served two years as the cook, her own three small children at her side in the kitchen. Later, she took a job as a nurse's aide in a surgery unit where she found the "visual opportunities of looking into all those opened bodies fascinating."

Intense and thoughtful observation of the physical world is the impetus of Yoder's art. Much of her abstract, angular work describes the essential elements of her terrain. She drives three days a week through the countryside to Iowa City where she manages the print study room at the University's Museum of Art. The twenty-mile drive has filled her studio bulletin board with photos of fence rows, doorways, intersections of lines and light. The images are starting points for her imagination, spark to the flint, but are rarely recognizable in her finished work.

A small wooden building nestled kitty-corner from a barn is her studio. The ink plate is hot to the touch, the door handle black from her hands. A space heater takes off the chill. The heart of the studio is a treasured press, bought second-hand from a man she is sure regrets the day he let it go. Martha stands firmly planted at the four-foot press wheel and turns it hand-over-hand, the felt on the roller impressing ink from the plate to the paper.

To ease the tightness printmaking brings, Martha draws. Moving happily between the two media, a series of prints provides the energy for a series of collage drawings in oil pastels and graphite. She also paints and intends to return to canvas soon. "I need to augment my work." She wishes her studio had more light and room for an easel, but she will improvise, a master of using what is at hand.

$\backsim$ *Paddy Blackman*

Sally Stepanek

Sally Stepanek politely dodges my requests for a long-distance phone interview. I insist she's not playing fair. She's a writer, she knows the routine. Writers interview subjects and then create stories. Sally e-mails to Robbie in capital letters. "I'm TERRIBLE at on-the-spot interviews," she pleads through the keyboard from her home in New York City. "Deer in the headlights."

Her mother has recently died. I am sympathetic but persistent. I fax her the same short list of questions I've posed in conversation with nine other artists, hoping for written responses I can cut and paste into a portrait. She calls Robbie, saying this won't work either. She would be writing forever.

Once I give Sally's wishes the attention they deserve, the more I question my own motives, my urge to make narrative out of arbitrary ingredients. I feel this portrait project expand to reach our needs. What can we learn about the lifework of an artist from what she has left behind? I study Robbie's photograph of their afternoon in Tipton as if it were a passport into Sally's years in Iowa.

Like this enigmatic and ecstatic image, Sally's trail is elusive and intense. I find news coverage about her sixty-three-mile "meditative path" circling the Iowa City countryside, an art installation called "21 Doors." I imagine the footprints of walkers as the dotted lines between the twenty-one steel doorframes she planned to set in concrete. I reread her interviews with artists in *Tractor* magazine, remembering how they had caught my attention when they first appeared. Mutual friends tell me about her altered books, including a photo album, *For Your Imagination's Memory*.

Two months pass, then an express mail package from Sally arrives at my house. I study what she has chosen for me, still hunting for clues. It is mostly recent work; none of the things I've found in Iowa are included. I unfold oversize photocopies of her assessments of other artists published in the Czech Republic English-language arts and book review, a newspaper column she co-created with Czech editor Marie Chribková for the past year in Prague. I read her *Poems to Seize Sound*, printed in an edition of three copies, and excerpts from her book-length poem, *Three, Breathing*. She publishes her creative writing under several different pseudonyms, and I wonder about the river between the person and the persona in poetry.

Leafed in with these materials, I stop at a compelling message. "I'm working on a new book, *The Glyptic*, a dialogue between a woman and God—an argument modeled, of course, on the Book of Job but also an extended rage against certain narrative traditions," Sally comments. "If I were to write anything about art-making and writing, I'd have to describe my understanding of prayer and worship. But words about such things are as difficult to find as their actual practice—especially after a loss."

꙳ *Marianne Abel*

Emily Martin

Walking through Emily Martin's studio is like threading your way among the crowded booths of a festival market. Stacks of chrome-framed paintings and sculpted towers line the shelves, and handmade books and rolls of frosted mylar fill the waist-high counters. A book press is stashed under a table. Four family parakeets are chirping, the dog Gomez is barking, and the air conditioner is humming in the workplace of this painter, printmaker, and book artist.

There are "people" too, in her studio, figures distinctly Emily Martin's and used in much of her work. She came to these figures in graduate school. She was working with a variety of images, one a disembodied head. Heads required bodies when Emily's work became more narrative. Because stick figures were too slim to be noticed, she "fattened them up." Her simple figures have no hair, no clothes, and no identifiable gender or age. "I want these figures to stand for every human being," she says, "and to be noticed for their position and gesture rather than quirks of personality."

The design of the figures has led some viewers into the facile belief that Emily's work is simply humorous. The artist is saying much more. In "It Isn't Always Funny," the story of a problem relationship is told through figures sitting slumped at a table and drinking from a bottle. The figures are studied in a rondo of sixteen color-photocopied scenes painted specifically to be rearranged and re-combined. The right half of one scene is also the left half of the next, although the images are repeated with variations in color. The rondo is complete when the last scene repeats an image from the first. "I wanted to address the ups-and-downs of relationships," says Emily, "where problems are often without resolution."

Emily's signature figures also inhabit the pages of her books. *House Detective* is an accordion house of black-and-white photocopies featuring crime and romance. Each page depicts a moment or scene. Folding the pages in different combinations, we can create our own stories.

Emily has always made books. She began with a sketchbook, and now has an expanded collection of ideabooks, the pages holding as many words as images. "It is logical for me to be a book artist," she says, "because books always suggest words even if you don't use them." Emily also makes books because they are inviting. We are used to handling books. We can open them. In fact, she defines a "book" as anything that opens, including pieces that others may define as sculptural, such as her *Safety Manual.* She revels in the interaction of words and images as they are arranged and rearranged. Emily Martin provides a festival of ways of seeing and saying in renewed abundance.

Paddy Blackman

Joan Soppe

Joan Soppe offers art that must be "seen" with the hands as well as the eyes. Her handmade books are designed to be held. To explore her work you must turn each page and, reading the text and studying the design, you also feel compelled to run your fingertips along the metal relief, or open the tiny door in the middle of a page, or remove an embedded box to discover that it, too, opens and is filled with small treasures.

Awkward Peeping, a book concerned with gender and abuse, reveals one page in which an old prescription box is set. When you pry out the box and open it, you shake out a small pink hairbrush and a baby bottle. That event becomes yours to interpret.

Bookmaking is an expansion and extension of Joan's drawing method. She draws in three dimensions using small new and found objects, as well as metal she has cast and paper she has made. She has also studied printmaking and woodworking. "I learn as much as I can. They all add to my tool box."

Her spacious three-room studio called "Nom de Plume" is in an old brick building on a quiet, tree-canopied street in Cedar Rapids. Each room is anchored by a large, waist-high table covered with clean white paper. Here Joan constructs her books, some in limited editions and others as one-of-a-kind.

Joan believes artists must reach out to the community. She teaches both bookmaking and bookbinding to adults and children. And she markets her own work faithfully. "It never hurts to have a book available to sell," she says as she wedges a book into her purse. "People aren't going to come to me. I have to go to them."

As she leans over the worktable in her studio, Joan's slender hand reaches gracefully toward *Dos à Dos*, a book which opens at either side. "I like the shape of a circle," she confides, "because like *Dos à Dos*, it has no beginning and no end."

Paddy Blackman

Starla Stensaas

As I came to know Starla Stensaas, I learned of her training as a poet and a weaver, her work as a faculty member in college art departments, and as a graphic designer. She was constantly making connections between graphic design, desktop publishing, papermaking, and artist-made books. Watching her at work on a number of a book's constituent parts—making paper, tinkering with one turn of a phrase in a poem, setting text on her computer, arranging scanned images and applying color to them, and preparing a book for exhibition—I have become intrigued by the ways her art crosses aesthetic boundaries. Indeed, her art is energized and driven by the effort to cross all sorts of boundaries.

Arms elbow deep in paper pulp, Starla screws up her face. Watching her, I am aware of my own face beginning to scrunch with distaste. I am thinking of my mother mashing the weekly meatloaf, and how it felt to stick my hands into that raw cold glop. Stensaas has different associations. "Papermaking as a process for me is related to gardening, bread-making, yogurt-making, and laundry. In the ways I approach it, it is women's work. Like hanging wash outside, the sheets of paper hang from the clothesline. Like baking bread, it requires stages of preparing pulp. Like yogurt-making, you wait overnight for it to be ready. Like composting, or preparing a meal, you use leftovers in different ways," she explains. The connection to women's work is deliberate, one of many she has worked, with much tenacity, to foreground in her art and integrate into her life.

A crucial point in Stensaas' development came in 1984 with a stay at Kate Millett's farm/studio in New York. Millett's work, integrating feminist and female-centered images and language, helped Starla envision art which meshed the visual and the verbal in new ways. "Here was one of my favorite feminist writers using text like poetry, then placing it in a fine arts context," she recalls. At this cooperative women's community, working to create living space, studio space, and art, she also found a model for aesthetic living rooted in feminist values.

In 1987, inspired by poet Galway Kinnell's "The Bear," she made *Crossing the Broken Arrow Expressway to Bear*, based on an old Indian and Eskimo myth. Bear, a powerful magic animal, symbolizes an important spiritual union between human hunter and animal prey. Stensaas recasts the myth from a technological and materialistic viewpoint which includes the I Ching, Dian Fossey's gorillas, and Cruise missiles. Using xerography and laser typography on Japanese papers, she juxtaposes old and new technologies in both the content and form.

"Because the dualism of the old myth is re-created in the poem," she explains, "a dualism is likewise set up in the form of the book." The medium and materials—codex with hand-made papers, and choices made in binding—evoke a pre-printing press work or a holy book. In contrast, the digital form of the text, on computer disk in a front pocket designed as the book's endpaper, "speaks to technology and materialism, and negates the one-of-a-kind holy book by creating the possibility of endless copies of the text." Stensaas exhibits a computer with the book, inviting visitors to print the poem.

Among women's communities with whom Stensaas has worked and lived, she continues to cross boundaries, seeking a vision and commitment to a holistic aesthetic and an aesthetic life.

᪥ *Laura Julier*

Leola Bergmann

We're just about the same height. Our hair is just about the same shade of gray. Our friends would describe us as trim, but Leola and I glance down at our slightly rounded bellies and share a commiserating grin. She is eighty-three, and I am just over thirty years younger, but in our conversation on her breezy porch there's a moment when I know I want to be like her when I grow up.

Perhaps it's that moment when she shows me how osteoporosis can be met and managed so that flexibility returns and work resumes. Or that moment when I begin to believe that one can make a good life alone after shepherding one's deeply-loved husband through his final illness. Then again, it may be her evocation of the pleasures of having grandchildren nearby, or the furry companionship of two pet cats who calmly take for granted that sometimes we humans pace from room to room and think out loud. Or it's the pause to savor evidence that our work is appreciated and worth sharing.

In Leola's case, for example, prints requested by the editor for the covers of three recent issues of the *Iowa Review*. Her 1994 retrospective show by invitation from ARTS IOWA CITY. Her speech just delivered at the Iowa State Fair Sesquicentennial chautauqua

because her 1948 book, *The Negro in Iowa*, reprinted in 1968, was the first study devoted to the history of our state's black citizens. Her interdisciplinary University of Iowa Ph.D. dissertation on St. Olaf College choralmaster F. Melius Christiansen published years before American Studies officially came into being, and reprinted in 1968. And a commission to research and publish *Americans from Norway* in 1950, later reprinted in a series that anticipated the current intellectual fervor for ethnicity studies.

Now we're up and walking through the house. The inside wall of a narrow porch has been removed to create a light-filled eating space. Freed-up windows open toward shady gardens maintained with help Leola hired after her clear-eyed look at what she must rearrange for life ahead. A new white-tiled bathroom, eked out of closet and formal dining space on the main floor, will afford extra convenience for Leola's future in the family house. After years of making-do in gloom and old grit, Leola converted her basement to a pristine studio for work and storage after she began to live and work alone at home. Leola's work continues, since she's eager with each turn of the wheel to see how the next image will turn out. Her favorite results hang on her walls beside the works of younger printmakers she has encouraged.

How can she do all this? It seems to me that Leola has always pursued her intellectual, creative, and practical questions without regard for fad or formula. She has done this alongside her loved ones, and has persisted on her own after they have left. She can face change. She can make a life as pioneering as it is palimpsestic. And can I—will I—do it, too? I watch Leola wave hello to two young men who have arrived to help her with computer work as soon as she has waved good-bye to me. Turning toward home, I grant myself a good thirty years to try.

                                   Carol Lauhon

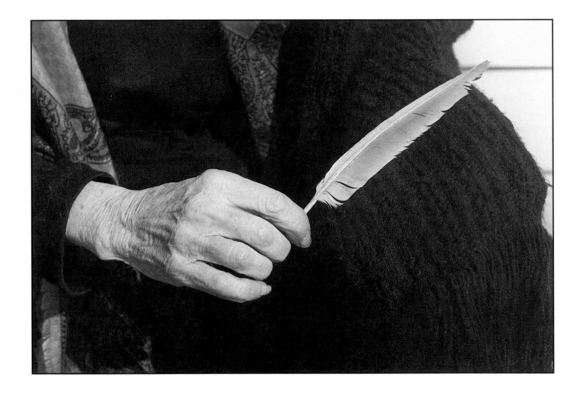

Tenting Together

As her writer/editor and friend in several projects, I support Robbie Steinbach's 3-D vision. Her photographic portraits make conspicuous the strength and beauty of women artists. Work by each artist-subject is also included, undeniable evidence of the creative agency of the woman herself. Coming along third are brief essays—accompanying the visual production and aspiring to provide another view of the artist's life and work. But I know, I know.... Unless I'm your mother or your daughter, or you are the artist-subject of one of my word portraits, you aren't paging through principally to see what I myself have to say. In fact, with a title here and a date there to help you identify the splendid visual work you're encountering, I suspect you wouldn't even miss me. Thus I'm tempted to be flashy, or easy, or maybe so packed with authority that you feel compelled to read this whole essay to the end.

I'll simply bare two bones of the task we took on, the other writers and I, when we said we'd help Robbie realize her vision. First of all, our writer's questions on your behalf were feminist, although some of the women we engaged in conversation might insist that they are artists first and women second, as if the two identities were not in any way related to how they got here. Some speak as if they arrived in spite of obstacles. Some, because of obstacles. Others will not recall obstacles at all. But here they are, gathered together. "Women." That label is as smooth as the covers of this book. Divergent politics are tenting together. When you pull aside the covers you expose gender reference to the light for a moment. You pause to ask: How does it matter to you that this work you're seeing is by women only?

The other bone is that, as receptive interviewers, we've heard the assumption that our essays would be fitted comfortably to the artists' sense of self like wool slippers formed to their feet. Instead, inspired by their personal histories, we'd sometimes rather make our essays into patent leather tap shoes of our own, with grosgrain bows. We've felt inspired to show off. But workers as we are in nonfiction prose, that extra dimension in Robbie's vision, we writers know that our talent works best sometimes in shaping inconspicuously the material we've been given, material important to the artist, material which helps to answer the questions you came in with. We confess to having indulged ourselves in a metaphor here or there, and even in thematic resonance, however subdued. We couldn't help it. Our admiration for all you see between these covers made us do it. I expect you'll understand.

෴ *Carol Lauhon*

Marilyn Annin

The sculpted garments, bright in silk, aluminum can tabs, lace, and bottle caps, stand like people at a social gathering. Alone or in a small group, they are the center of the room, the charismatic personality that draws a crowd. Marilyn Annin's sculpture, "His Precious Jewel," seems to clothe a young woman. She wears a patchwork dress with flying shoulder straps, the small bodice centered by a silver star. Move closer, engage this fascinating creature in conversation. The dress is pieced from men's neckties and detailed with a chain of can tabs. The star is a cookie cutter.

We toss, and Marilyn collects, amassing plastic six-pack holders, zippers, buttons, safety pins. "I think can tabs are beautiful. They are well designed, lightweight, strong. They are like a key."

You would never guess that Marilyn is a collector by walking through her uncluttered living space. She works at a table set simply in a corner of glass windows. On the table sits a torso, a skeleton of welded quarter-inch steel rods, the armature for her sculptures. She meticulously wraps the steel in cloth, then sews the fabric directly onto the frame. In some pieces, the framework is hidden, in others it becomes part of the work.

"The hardest thing to do is to get rid of something good in my art." As a painter and weaver, she learned the discipline of choice, but she leaves the meaning and metaphor of her work open. The three "Sandbag Women" grew out of the 1993 Des Moines River flooding. Annin began the series while the helicopters were flying over her house delivering sandbags. She stitched unused bags into the figures' garments. The sandbags, as precious as jewels during the flood, became useless and contaminated garbage abandoned at the river's edge when the water subsided.

Marilyn reflects, "Through the centuries women have found pleasure in reworking leftover bits and pieces and making them into something special for others to enjoy—quilts, casseroles, or in my case, sculptured garments."

♪ *Paddy Blackman*

Helen Kerrigan, BVM

The fourth floor studio office is quiet and bright, the door open. Sister Helen Kerrigan, sitting at her desk in the corner, looks up when I knock. Her gray eyes wait for me to declare myself.

Sister Helen takes her time. She has a ritual for her work in oil. First she meticulously arranges a model, such as the small glass jar filled with marbles placed in front of a draped white handkerchief on the studio counter. Both the model and her sturdy paint-spattered easel are arranged to catch the sun slanting through the large window. Angles of light and reflections are important in her work. So is size. Though the model is four or five inches tall, the canvas is three by four feet. "I always paint from a model, which is generally very small, but my work is large."

The marbles, saved from her childhood, are swirls of colors, but their glossy surfaces carry tiny reflections. Scrutinize the painting in progress and you will see the studio's arched paneled window, the easel, the rectangular ceiling fixture in the curve of the painted spheres.

To combat the slow progress of her realistic work in oil, Sister Helen exercises by painting abstract art with acrylics. She studied and admires the abstract expressionists of the 1950s. She shares De Kooning's passion for the act of painting. When she works abstractly, she has no model. Instead, she paints as she goes, exploring the emotions created by the juxtaposition of shapes and colors. "The abstract expressionists considered painting an arena in which to act. I paint and then step back and study, deciding what to do next."

Sheer enjoyment prompts Sister Helen to create. She comes to her studio every day anxious to work. She has always felt like this about painting and drawing, even as a young girl when she was the only student among hundreds who took art at the Immaculate Conception Academy in Davenport. There her teacher and mentor was Sister Mary Blanche, an artist and member of the order of the Blessed Virgin Mary, BVM. Later, after two years at Clarke College, Sister Helen entered the convent, following both her mentor and her older sister. Later her younger sister followed her. Over forty years later, the three Kerrigan sisters, members of the same order, live together in Dubuque. All three work at Clarke College.

Sister Helen has taught and painted in the art department for thirty years. She loves to help beginning students learn to see. She sets a simple brown paper bag as a model for her students. "They are so wonderful to paint, to understand volume, light, and shading.

"Art is my life," Sister Helen declares. "I can't imagine not painting."

ᔣ *Paddy Blackman*

Astrid Hilger Bennett

Astrid Hilger Bennett has constructed a canvas coat of many lists. She can slip her arms into the sleeves and wear this coat, although it is hung as a piece of art. The cloth is a screenprinted collage of lists from the artist's daily life. The pockets hold booklets of personal insights from her journals, sketchbooks, and memory. The work is titled "AMULET COAT: Mother Art Journeys II."

"I would like to make a series of such works and have them worn on the streets where passers-by might take a second look. I want someone to say, 'Oh! That's on my list, too.' I want strangers to rummage in a pocket, take out a booklet, and read a line or two."

The motion and diversity of Astrid's life, belied by her patient gaze and measured bearing, express themselves in artwork as varied as her roles: fiber artist, violinist, retailer, daughter, wife, mother, friend, citizen, arts advocate, and lover of the natural world. She has created everything from printed tea cozies to large wall hangings. Her work is alive with bright colors and movement, the fabrics often screenprinted several times and then handpainted with dyes. She mixes techniques, exploring. Her violinist's sensibility infuses rhythm and patterning in her work. She employs images she has created and catalogued as a musician uses notes—in ever different combinations.

Astrid works in a small studio in the basement of her home. Her ten-foot-long worktable rests on a cement floor impervious to the spills of dyes, waxes, and painting processes. She yearns for more time in the studio, but balances that work with tending to three children and serving as part time manager of the Iowa Artisans' Gallery in Iowa City. She believes that "busy participation in life" provides a rich source of ideas for art, and her life is abundant with active creativity.

℘ *Paddy Blackman*

Naomi Schedl

Her coffee is strong and black. Her windows are tall and wide. Her house sits on an ancient bank of the Iowa River. As she talks, she gazes at the dark, leaf-lined ravine below and the wide, midwestern meadow on the other side.

Naomi Schedl came to Iowa City when her children were young. A painter with an M. F.A. from Yale, she studied printing and dyeing and began her lifework as a teacher. She learned weaving and basketry, and mentored students in fiber art who now teach and practice across the country. Her students, children, and grandchildren return often to the house in Iowa City.

A blackened cradle sits upright and empty, like an opened egg, like a singed vagina, on the floor of Naomi's studio. Its woven sides have been stiffened with sticks. A cloth the color of blood and ash makes a ragged puddle within the cradle's base. Naomi's cradle/casket series marks the site of a "scorched village." It bespeaks decimation of her native South Africa and on her adopted continent.

Interpreting cradle/caskets, then blankets, then fences, then ladders, Naomi has built a fourteen-foot-high ladder of tree branches, lining its steps with moon craters and naming it "Further Than the Eye Can See." Through blue-black terrain in oils on large canvases, a yellow river makes its crooked way. Other upright canvas riverbeds are blue-black and viscous, their corners clogged by wax indigo leaves. On the floor, a riveted river of metal plates is banked by more dead leaves. Naomi installs warnings: Look what is before us to celebrate and to mourn.

ଇ *Carol Lauhon*

Isabel Bloom

Isabel Bloom's sculptures of children and animals share a roundness that must be caressed. Viewers cup a hand and follow the smooth concrete curve of the back of a child's head or a crouched rabbit.

"I like simple things. And roundness." She began selling clay sculptures at a local art fair, then she took some along to Chicago and a gallery ordered a few. The demand for her work grew. She responded by making molds and reproducing her work in quantity. Increased production meant the need for more work space. Her father bought her the Eleventh Street studio where her work is still sold in Davenport. "He built all the shelves in the studio," Bloom remembers.

Though married to an artist, John Bloom, she does not call herself one. "So bohemian, you know," she says with a laugh. They met as residents at Grant Wood's artist colony in Stone City, Iowa. She insists her impulse to sculpt emanates from the practical desire to "pick up a little extra cash." The community loves her commercial work. She creates her commissioned work—a life-sized girl reading a book for a local library garden, a woman with a child at her skirt standing in a hospital entranceway—by layering concrete on a wire frame. The process takes time, strength, and stamina. Today these are in short supply, as Bloom battles Parkinson's disease. She works with an assistant and together they develop ideas and collaborate on pieces.

Relationships are the center of Isabel's life. She sits in a chair by the window of her Mississippi River bluff home, her white hair pinned in waves, and in a soft voice tells stories from her long, productive life. Her eyes crinkle up in laughter often as she recalls anecdotes about her husband and three sons. "People who don't have a family don't know what they're missing," she declares. She once had a TV show demonstrating art projects for children. She used her own projects on the show to demonstrate egg decorating, and once, as she talked into the camera, her children ate every single egg. "I don't remember how I recovered from that."

Isabel's varied interests and projects mingle with play. A son gave her a remote-control car that she guides around the living room floor. She delights in a wind-up chicken as it hops on orange plastic feet in front of her chair. "Wind it up again," she urges.

Wonder took her to Russia three times, traveling alone in the days when few women did. She immersed herself in Russian frescoes and mosaics and ventured lunch with four Georgian girls. "My diary records that we communicated by gesture and had a wonderful time."

The Blooms have lived in just two houses in their fifty-four years together. They still live in the second house, a place overflowing with treasures, stories, and the energy and spirit these artists devote to shaping their surroundings. Isabel believes in art which has "soul, a feeling that wakes you up."

ᔐ *Paddy Blackman*

Gloria Zmolek

"I couldn't be an artist until I got rid of the notion that I had to impress people," Gloria Zmolek explains. "I thought artists were special people and I wasn't one of them." Challenges come in so many forms that she isn't always sure what she resists. Is it the self-doubt she learned from her mother growing up in Ames? Or is it society's low expectations of women? Sometimes her Catholic upbringing stalls a decision—is she doing enough for others? She throws the heap of cultural laundry aside. "I've learned that artists are just like everyone else. There are prima donnas in all fields. I like the people who are just out there, like me—what you see is what you get."

Her art frequently explores these hierarchies of value. Asked to create a self-portrait for a group show, she felt stumped at first. "My son was into baseball at the time, so I was into baseball." She quilted a tabernacle of baseball players photo-transferred from her son's card collection onto handmade paper rectangles. A top triangle of larger, fancier cards enshrines the better players. The others line up in rows, everyone conformed into the same tight frames. Bows tied through the piece record the judgement that hand-sewn quilts are better than others. "An artist's life is a lot like a baseball player's," she laughs. Gloria's card takes its place in the line-up. "Few of us realize much money or fame, but at least we're all doing something we're passionate about."

She taught art in public schools until she chose to stay home with her two infants, born fifteen months apart. She was sure this informal leave of absence would end with a new teaching job. One Saturday she took a watercolor class with Iowa artist Jo Myers-Walker. During the workshop's last hour, Jo showed the class how she recycled her unsatisfactory or unsellable watercolors by stuffing shreds into a blender to make new pulp. "When I used to hear artists say that 'I do it because I have to,'" Gloria recalls, "I never understood what they meant until I met paper."

Paper is her medium, and she delights in what can only be expressed through its unique qualities. "I'd like to see where I can take the sheet," she says. Passion is more important to her than being prolific. In "Follow Your Bliss," she wove dollar bill strips with other fibers. "Papermaking was a gift to me." Yet producing art to make money conflicted with her joy in creativity. "Being my own boss can be good, but it can control my life more than if I had a job. Why let art control my life?"

Until her children leave home in a few years, she sets her daily compass by her teenagers' needs. "My work now is with my kids. It's where I get most of my inspiration." Though she and her husband have recently divorced, they set an example of being self-employed, doing work they love, for years. "We preferred to give our kids experiences." When Gloria complains about the difficulties, her daughter chides, "Mom, follow your bliss."

In 1995, Gloria self-published *Teaching Hand Papermaking: A Classroom Guide*, to reach future teachers. She claims she "never had the courage to be an artist." Producing and marketing the book has become a yardstick. She didn't think of herself as a risk-taker either, but she has exceeded many expectations. She folds her paper tiles at committee meetings, taking the work with her wherever she goes.

෴ *Marianne Abel*

Sheryl Ellinwood

Sheryl Ellinwood's studio is the egg of her artistic life, holding both the yolk of her sculptural work and the white heat of glassblowing. The large structure of gray steel nestles among tall trees on the southeast shore of Lake Red Rock.

The artist sees herself as "a sculptor who happens to blow glass." September through May, glass smolders twenty-four hours a day in a computer-controlled furnace, waiting at 2000 degrees Fahrenheit for Sheryl's breath to give it shape and volume. She has built her equipment: the furnace, the annealers, and the glory hole, all deployed like sentinels along one wall of the studio. Shelves are lined with her color-swirled paperweights, fish that swim in air, and vessels in cobalt blue. Glassblowing, something Ellinwood tried on a dare, has provided her with a living since her undergraduate days.

A separate room in the studio holds the welding equipment for her true calling. For three months of each year, Sheryl shuts down the glass furnace to concentrate all her attention on her mixed media sculpture. She has found she needs a solid block of time with no distractions to complete pieces which satisfy her.

Just as Sheryl has arranged two spaces and two seasons to separate her glassblowing and sculpting, her cat Smooch has been provided with two beds in the studio, one for summer and one for winter. At the center of the structure, however, upholstered chairs are drawn up where visitors can gather to relax and feel at home.

Home—the house form and its arrangements—is a central interest in the artist's recent work. Called "Private Parts," a house form with a hinged door displays a headless doll seated in a central niche. On the wallpaper behind the doll is printed the definition of "privacy." The viewer-as-reader experiences the unsettling self-consciousness of viewer-as-voyeur. Sheryl's message is one of protest and protectiveness. "The house form," she says, "is a symbol of ego-less self, being, soul, spirit, essence."

Under one roof and produced by one artist, glassblowing and mixed media sculpting enhance the expressive potential of one practice for the other. Nevertheless, while glassblowing supports the artist, it is her sculpting which sustains her, and endures.

ↄ *Paddy Blackman*

Mary Snyder Behrens

"Ideally, I prefer not to talk about it," Mary Snyder Behrens says of her artwork. "After all, I'm a *visual* artist." When she responds to gallery visitors' questions, she offers conversation about the how and why and leaves the meaning on the wall. "Whatever anything means, evolves." The time and place the piece was made, where it is shown or exhibited, the day the piece is seen and who sees it—many factors influence interpretation. She trusts the audience, even when they fear their own opinions. "It's common for people to be apprehensive about looking at art," she says, "but I still don't think it's the artist's responsibility to explain the work."

Feeling responsibility to create art is enough of a challenge. "I'm involved in making a commodity that people neither need nor want. I'm always asking myself what's worth doing, and why should I do it." Months of depression can separate her from a creative spurt. When ideas come, she works furiously, knowing the energy won't last long. "Everything else in my life falls apart." Often, she finds a concept that will carry her through a series, like her recent "Stations," or a new project on St. Theresa, themes that help her assess her Catholic upbringing.

"Ultimately, I think art is about making relationships, about finding connections," Mary says about how patterns help us focus. Growing up in Milwaukee, she created landscapes and yards for her dolls, telling stories about imaginary communities. She sewed her own clothes, and later turned to punk. Yearning to become an artist, she waitressed her way through art school. She tried oil paintings and then gouaches. Punk in college was also collage, a form that kept creeping back into her work.

She steers her abstract fiber paintings toward the periphery of vision where she can reach the blurred edge of intense feeling. "Just because my work is not specifically representational doesn't mean that it lacks content." Mixing media helped Mary "make associations on the picture plane" that satisfied her fascination with patterns, textures, and objects. Chocolate swirled cookies became targets. Only a dotted line remains of the candy canes she used to cut out of magazines and paste onto her work. She thinks of the thread in her sewing machine as paint.

An arts advocate and volunteer, she feels frustrated by what many artists experienced as a crash in the market during the nineties, topped by a hostile gallery climate. "The arts are so approachable, so accessible," she says. "It's such an honest living, making art or writing. Nothing's more honest than that. And when it's written up as an elitist activity, it makes it even harder for the artist to make a connection with the public."

On the other hand, "I'm not one of those people who thinks my art is everything." An avid gardener and cook, Mary recently completed her first season as a vendor at the Waterloo/Cedar Falls farmers' markets. She experiments with all kinds of life. "I love putting things together that aren't ordinarily together." After nourishing others with her organic vegetables and exotic breads, she looks forward to a productive winter in her Dysart studio.

∽ *Marianne Abel*

Sheila Shumaker Mesick

Sheila Mesick sits at her desk in a junior high art room after school and tells how she got there. Her grandmother taught her to see geraniums in the moonlight. Her mother allowed her to draw on bedroom walls. Her father's sensitivity helped her express her personal feelings. The death of her husband, Paul Shumaker, her high school art teacher to whom she was married for eight and one-half years, propelled her into painting and teaching.

"The subject matter I deal with—women beset by drastic changes—is not comfortable to live with," Sheila says. "People ask why I paint what I do, and I think of the women in my family who were steadfast and nurturing but didn't express themselves or their feelings freely. I deal with whatever is at hand—human issues."

In one of her paintings, a woman with plum-colored hair dreams snails of color. In another, a white-faced woman backgrounded by painted hands holds a broken pot.

Of her nudes she says, "I usually show breasts, which I see as nurturing. Breasts are the symbol of where life comes from. In expressing deep emotion, the hand goes to the breast."

Her painting started, she says, "when everything was taken away from me—when Paul died—I had to basically find out who I was."

Now married to a high school classmate, Charles Mesick, she is in a "transitional state" in trying to get away from the motif of the female figure. "I want to start working smaller, doing highly-patterned still lifes, like fabric. I love pattern and color. I'd like to get into nature painting, too.

"I think about things a lot, conjuring images and stirring the pot. When it's ready, it's ready."

☙ *Julie Jensen McDonald*

Sharon Burns-Knutson

She doesn't know whether her kids think she's different because she's an artist. Sharon seems ordinary enough. She coaches the soccer team. She lives with her husband, an IRS auditor, and their two sons in Cedar Rapids. She runs and cross-country skis around neighborhood parks, trailing an enthusiastic black dog named Annabelle. She teaches elementary school art classes part-time in Iowa City, where she was born and raised. She goofs off and giggles a lot.

Sharon paints the subtleties that flutter on the surface of life, obvious things she thinks anyone can see. When giving me directions to her place, she assured me that I'd recognize her blue house because I'd seen it in "Moving Blues," her painting  about moving from an old house she'd loved to this suburban setting. The painting is a psychically-charged collage of brilliantly colored stars and symbols and staircases, cats and hearts and girls. I'm sure the blue house is in there, but it was a lot easier to find "number thirty-five in the middle of the block on the right."

"I paint quiet stories, little home stories that maybe everybody has." In "Five More Dracula Years," and many other paintings, she records the conflicts and sorrows of parenting adolescents. One son has dressed as Dracula for every Halloween since he was four. He has outgrown the costume and the holiday, but the persona remains. Loud, grungy music blasts the windows. The house cries tears. In another painting about a family vacation to Colorado, she depicts herself as a hen, a radiant red chicken. "Don't I ever paint happy things? Well, there's a rainbow in there."

She admires petroglyphs and collects many kinds of tribal and folk art from wooden masks to animal figurines and beaded belts that are scattered like amulets throughout the house. Images of these artifacts surface in her paintings. "I pick up images all the time," she laughs. "Might as well share the good stuff." She can explain the events and feelings that provide the source material for her works, but she'd rather not stop viewers' curiosity there. "It's better if a person makes up their own story."

She tapes a sheet of jet-black printer's paper to a cardboard sheaf when she's ready to start a new painting. She props it on her easel beside the big living room window facing the street. She likes the light there. Sharon stashes a tray of oil paints and brushes underneath the sofa's sidetable, perhaps a small acknowledgement that maybe her approach to life isn't so ordinary after all.

～ *Marianne Abel*

Ben Sunday

"I knew when I was four that I was an artist," Ben Sunday says. "There was no doubt in my mind." Years later she formulated her definition of art with her late husband, calligrapher Joe Dain: "Art is intuitive transcendence of master craftsmanship."

In her long experience of making and teaching art, materials and techniques have been the learnable and teachable things. The artist-within she discovered at age four is not teachable, she believes. "All you can teach is materials and technique. Knowledge in those is the basis of everything I have contributed to artists." Yet, "craftsmanship is not enough. You have to be able to apply the technical skill and come out with something that approaches art."

Ben is always looking for "that mystery, that presence" that makes art more than materials. "Our life experience is more than science can explain. I try to reach into the unexplained and express it in some way."

There's a resonance of ancient wisdom in her paintings and collages. Early and late. Recent works are handmade paper of glowing color in collages with larger forms. Of one, "Artifact," Ben says, "I am breaking into a great old wall in an archaeological expedition. I find things as I go into the wall."

Ben Sunday cultivates an extensive herb garden. Sage, chamomile, or thyme—herbs with piquant names—enhance flavors, heal, and sometimes cast a spell. Her paintings, from figurative to the abstract, perhaps can do the same.

ᢒ *Julie Jensen McDonald*

Nina de Creeft Ward

In a life drawing class Nina Ward took in college in Claremont, California, over thirty-five years ago, students drew the model and his dog. The assignment helped Nina acknowledge her talent in portraying animals. "The guy looked like he died there, and the dog looked great." She literally grew up with animals. Her mother kept a small dairy goat herd, and the milking parlor was a section of the large kitchen. Livestock and pets roamed nearly as freely as Nina through the house and yard.

Both her parents were artists. Her father lived in New York City but Nina grew up with her mother and grandmother in California, strong people who proved that "women can do anything." Her mother carved portraits of famous animals in wood, stone, and bronze. Now Nina expresses her own sensitivity for "the fragility of life" in etchings, paintings, prints, and fiber, ceramic, and mixed-media sculptures.

In her current exhibition, "Rhino/Blaauwbock Project," she shows how people have "caused a scourge to the balance of nature." Painted ammunition boxes, museum drawers, steamer trunks, and hat boxes decorated with travel souvenirs overflow with exotic animal parts. "I want to make a statement about anti-complacency," she says. "I think it's important to think about death. Something physical will put your mind on it whether you want to think about it or not. If you see something dead, you think about it." Visitors rush out of galleries. Her representations of extinct and endangered species resemble corpses strewn on the carpeted floor.

These might be the same people who buy Nina's whimsical animals at craft shops and summer fairs. Public taste produces the apparent contradiction between her large-scale environmental installations and the domesticated animals she crafts by the dozen to support her studio. "I know a lot of these things aren't serious, but serious things don't sell."

Her ark of glazed raku figures includes rabbits, pigs, chickens, horses, lambs, goats, and an occasional crèche set complete with donkeys. With gift-giving in mind, Nina captures a moment or gesture, even if a singing pig stretches the imagination to a pleasant edge. She creates each one as deliberately and spontaneously as a potter would fill an order for a score of bowls. "Art is a contemplative work. If I think too much, I can't do it." Nina spends days studying and drawing live animals at farms and zoos.

Figuring out what she needs to make her art has been as much of a process as the work itself. She overcame "the Eeyore syndrome" long enough to buy a cottage on the other side of Cedar Falls away from her husband and their five children. "One of the hardest things was separating from the family and the family's concerns." She let the kids play there first, then consulted a psychologist to help her accept the studio as her own space.

Nina thought that with such an investment she must produce something equal to Rodin or Picasso. The counselor suggested she just sit there and drink tea. "I'm not sure that my work is important to anyone else but me," she learned, "but it is important to me."

ᔓ *Marianne Abel*

Sarah Jane Boyd

Through the natural contours of impressed body prints, Sarah Jane Boyd extends artistic expression. "One image dries and I put another image on it. No one in the Quad Cities is doing this type of art."

In her personalized performance art, she pours water-based ink on a mattress topped with newsprint. She rolls her model across the paper. The soft surface allows the paper to envelop the body. "By rolling the model into the mattress you get a wonderful reprint like a fingerprint."

As a child Sarah Jane watched her mother paint delicate designs on china. She herself preferred scissors and paste. "I was always making things for people. My closet was probably my first studio."

Now she works by the open doors of a garage overlooking the Mississippi River, or while in her classroom at St. Katherine's-St. Mark's School.

Sarah Jane is partial to no artistic medium. "I enjoy what I'm doing at the time. But I probably like batik best because the piece is so involved. I crank a lot of them out for no other reason than that I like doing the work."

In batik, she manipulates cloth, wax, and dyes. Recessed color flows across a cratered canvas. Batik crosses the line from craft to art. "I don't worry about where the designs come from anymore. They're always there."

∽ *Teresa Ruzic*

Amy Worthen

A small scroll of metal rolls ahead of the burin. Engraver Amy Worthen grips the tool firmly. When the incision is complete, she leans back on her stool and brushes away the excised copper. Engraving is exacting and arduous work.

As a printmaker, Amy uses intricate and detailed architectural forms, sometimes mingled with nature, to explore ideas and events. "House Destroyed by Fire," an engraving of the charred and broken beams of a burned structure, was invoked by personal experience. Viewers follow a melancholy path among the ruins.

Architecture is visual literature, and Amy studies the spaces created by structure. Exploration of exteriors provides an opportunity for probing interior spaces, the stories and emotions housed within the structures she creates.

Duality is part of Worthen's life and art. She works as both an artist and art historian. Her seventy-year-old Des Moines home includes a lower level three-room studio dedicated to printmaking, and a first floor study and library for research and writing. Most years she divides her time between Des Moines and Italy where she teaches and studies. Recently in Venice, she produced "Sotoporteghi Veneziani," (Venetian Passageways), a limited edition book without text. Twelve engravings depict covered passageways, unique configurations of space, places that viewers can imagine both traveling and reflecting on the journey. The edition printing took place at Stamperia del Tintoretto, located in the studio of the sixteenth century painter.

"I wish I was more productive," Amy laments, detailing the nine months she invested in "Impossible Structure," a rich and involved engraving of architectural and entangled plant forms. In her studio she chronicles the evolution and history of the work. First conceived in a sketch book, the plate became increasingly dense as the drawings and prints matured.

Engraving is physically and mentally demanding. Her mentor, Leonard Baskin, taught her that an artist can be an intelligent whole person and warned her to "shun that which flows but does not bleed."

᠀ *Paddy Blackman*

Jan Friedman

Jan Friedman lives in a garden of fabric and yarn. Silk ribbons in flat baskets look like flower petals of greens and purples, pinks and blues. Skeins of yarn in gradations of purple or azure fill rectangular baskets which surround Jan's two large looms like floral beds around a grassy space. Wooden trees hold spools of yarn on their outstretched branches. Two more studio looms as well as two portable enough for demonstrations at fairs and community gatherings claim space throughout the house Jan shares with her husband and five-year-old daughter.

Mornings find Jan at work on linear tapestries. Most of her fiber art explores natural gradations of color. Flat areas progressing from dark to light are interrupted by nubby areas of woven silk. Afternoons and evenings in the company of her family, Jan sorts threads, winds warps, and produces her chenille scarves which sell so well at art fairs. When speaking on the phone, she takes up some preparatory task she has deliberately left beside it so that she can talk and work at the same time.

Preparatory work never ends, but it is a necessity this weaver relishes. She may unwind the ten filaments in a strand of yarn and replace one with a lighter shade of the same color. In the next strand, two filaments instead of one might be replaced for yet a new variation. The strands are neatly rolled and labeled for use in Jan's tapestries. She also hand-dyes silk and organza she later tears into ribbons for weaving. "Dyeing has never lost its magic for me. You never know how it will turn out." She tie-dyes fabric for color surprises, and sponge-dyes yarn.

Also collected are found objects—buttons, Japanese papers, additional fabrics, leaves, and old sewing patterns. Working recently with the idea of contentment/containment, Jan has combined some of her hoard of found objects with the "house form" in collages she values as articulations of personal ideas.

Jan Friedman's daily life moves with the rhythm she has generated at her loom. Tasks of living and working lap over and under one another, over and under, in a household pattern of not a single uncultivated moment.

☙ *Paddy Blackman*

Laurie Elizabeth Talbot Hall

The gendering of identity has a history which does not escape the scrutiny of Laurie Hall. The cloaking of her lifespace and yours and mine with instructions on how to be a girl and how to be a woman is so seamless that we've been liable to come to womanhood without coming to awareness. Of what is there to be aware? That the choices we believe we are exercising and the freedom we assume is ours have been swaddled in contingencies for generations leading up to the moment of our birth. Our mothers meant well. Their mothers meant well. And we continue to grow up by growing down to fit belittling spaces that cramp our style, spaces plastered with messages about beauty, delicacy, subordination, and suffering. Let's see the writing on the wall, says Laurie's work, and let's talk back.

Like wallpaper, prescriptions surround us, prescriptions we can't see as advertisements of our weakness. Drugs if you're dragging, since who'd love a woman who's a drag? Passes from Phys. Ed. class during that "time of the month." Rouge for a face drab with lack. Lack of autonomy, lack of the words to name the lack, lack of the means to set the record straight. And even in the aura of the silver screen, the full-lipped beauty yearns, a nimbus of shiny curls around her upturned face. Upturned for a kiss or a slap? Upturned for a pro- posal or abandonment? It's his call. It's been that way.

This is not good news. This is not an inspiring version of history. And yet, and yet. . . Here we are, attentive, tending to ourselves. And we are claiming for ourselves some time. Laurie reminds us to arrange our feminized, internalized histories for a good, hard look in the light. We're talking. We're listening, too, convinced that however tainted by contingencies unearned and unseen and unremarkable, our sense of things has always mattered.

Laurie's gone retro-, but she just might put uppity, funny lines in the cartoon balloons of the suffering star. A freeze frame of Ingrid Bergman's upturned face in *For Whom the Bell Tolls*, perhaps: "Saying yes to desire has a lot of implications." And by re-hanging vintage floral drapes, Laurie's helping us remember in those folds and petals our mothers' anxious, complicated love for us. By photographic imaging Laurie is exorcising old nightmares and fantasies to make a new room for dreams. And by plastering on gallery walls her wallpapers of prescriptions women grow up with, then learn however painfully to bring into awareness, Laurie invites us to go back in time and forward again, recall what we've been made to not-see, and struggle to re-word the claim to who it is we desire to become.

ᔦ *Carol Lauhon*

Ellen Wagener

Ellen Wagener tells time by the color of the sky. She has taught her six-year-old, too. Christopher tells her, "Come outside, it's the color of blue you love, the one right after dinner."

The color of the sky, the pattern of the clouds, the contour of the land are the elements of Ellen's Iowa landscapes. Her works are large. With pastel crayons, she recreates the familiar. Farmers, attracted to the accuracy and integrity of her work, stop to look and look again. "My mission as an artist is to present the ordinary in a way that avows majesty in quietness. I don't seek the spectacular."

Ellen smiles widely as she describes her passion for Iowa. She returned to her hometown, DeWitt, in 1990, a single parent knowing that, close to family, she and her son would flourish. She did not anticipate that her return would surround her with a new subject for her art. Her Iowa landscapes, selling well in New York City, support her life in the place she celebrates.

The sky dominates her art and shapes her life. Sunrise and sunset draw Ellen outside daily to drive the back roads in search of the subtle nuance, a pattern in the earth created by plows or a hue shared by land and sky. Finding what she has been looking for, Ellen clambers to the top of her van and snaps a photograph she will use as a study for her design.

Ellen believes that the beauty of the Iowa landscape contains the power to transform. "Recognizing the familiar in art energizes us to look again, to embrace the beauty we see every day."

෴ *Paddy Blackman*

Lucky the living child born in a land
Bordered by rivers of enormous flow

Paul Engle

Priscilla Steele

Being in a room with Priscilla Steele is like experiencing the subtle but powerful force of a riptide. She barely pauses for breath as she talks about how she has woven together art, teaching, and family. She doesn't apologize for being "indiscriminately ambitious." Her intense greenish eyes fix on you as she says, "I know this: I work the line well." And as she brushes away an errant strand of silver-shot hair, she adds, "Of course, it's often good to explore what you *don't* know." By the end of the conversation, Priscilla's diminutive frame somehow seems to have touched the most distant corner of her cavernous art gallery. Like a riptide, she has taken you where she wants to go, but not so far that you can't see where you've been.

Priscilla never flinches from looking backward or looking beyond. In fact, the full depth of her life as an artist, mother, wife, student, teacher, gallery owner, and theatre manager shapes her art.

"We live with our memories and our hopes. Even the most banal daily routine is colored by our regrets, our hopes, our morning pot of coffee." Periodically it all "blows up in my face," and even that is reflected in her art. Priscilla regrets letting go of only one piece, a lithograph depicting a volatile moment between a couple. The anguish and motion of the man and woman are universal without any breath of cliche. And that, she says, is the tough part—pulling off a wail without wailing.

As she strives to show people in all their complexity, Priscilla layers images or prints on both sides of the paper. Any one piece may be a melange of techniques, including intaglio, lithography, and photocopying.

A gifted teacher, Priscilla shows her students that art is more an active, spontaneous life process, not merely a premeditated act of control. As she draws in class, she tells them, "I'm failing right here, see? But I'm not going to erase. You can read a process only if you keep your mistakes." Although she willingly explores her weaknesses, Priscilla learned early to run with her strengths. Her prints are delicate evocations of nature and the human figure. With inspired legerdemain, she incises lines that convey not only motion but also depth and volume. Soft washes of color may be important, but she is in love with lines.

She learned this love at home. Her father had a naive love for drawing, and her mother believed humans were wonderful and capable of wonder. Just as Priscilla learned to cherish art from her life teachers, she has turned to pass on that love to her children, students, and fellow artists. She nurtures other people's triumphs. Her passion and her experience coalesce in the gallery, where she showcases the work of mostly Midwest artists. As in the early years when she sold her work beside other artists at small-town fairs, Priscilla now uses the gallery to reach out to the public.

"It's that translation of private experience, that forging of a bond between the artist and others, that so intrigues me. For any artist, it's a rare and shimmering moment when their work shows that human edge, that life force that makes people lean forward, catch their breath, and say, 'Oh, yes. I see.'"

✎ *Jean Florman*

Tilly Woodward

One wall of Tilly Woodward's reading room is covered with white. Here she has pinned up the paper for her work. A rain gutter lined with newspaper for catching chalk dust runs the length of the wall just above the baseboard. A small table holds her pastels, but there is no other evidence of an artist's studio in the house. "I have no time to go anywhere else. I want to be with my two children."

In the dining room hangs the familiar symbol of suffering, a portrait of Saint Sebastian. His hair is curled copper, his torso white. Shafts and vanes are the only hint of arrow tips buried beneath the pale skin. There is no blood, no torn flesh. No easy sentimentality. Just the steady, unflinching depiction of human woundedness. This life-sized work in chalk pastels is Tilly's.

Her art is nonfiction, her portraits those of real people. She began interpreting and drawing faces when she worked with juvenile felons at the McCune School for Boys in Kansas City. Tilly's portrait of Carl, an inner-city youth she worked with, hangs in her home. His dark eyes look tough but somehow vulnerable. "I compared Carl to Sebastian. Both were unacceptable to their societies, but one was seen as a saint and the other a criminal."

Tilly's most recent project is a series of portraits of Iowans who have AIDS or who are HIV-positive. The portraits are five feet by four feet. The faces of these mothers, brothers, and neighbors loom as large as the prospect of death which has entered their lives. Tilly visited each subject several times, drawing preliminary sketches and returning to seek their evaluation of her work. "If someone wanted a firmer chin or a clearer eye, I altered the sketch to reflect their view of themselves." The subjects could name themselves or remain anonymous. Many dictated words, an epitaph, perhaps, to be stenciled at the bottom of their portraits. Blonde-haired "Nancy" says: *What you send into the life of others comes back into your own. I am you.*

Acknowledging death, Tilly's portraits also celebrate life. She drew the faces of more than ninety residents of Dubuque, each nominated for acts of kindness or neighborliness during a time of racial violence and hatred. The portraits were displayed throughout the community to show that the caring spirit in Dubuque is real. Such portraits cannot be ignored. They are large and intimate evidence of the possibility for choosing to lead a loving life.

೪ *Paddy Blackman*

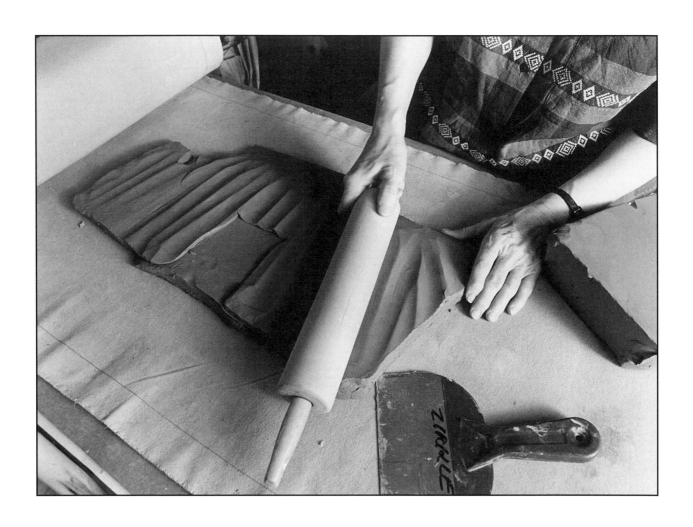

Merle Waller Zirkle

She's making her own clay these days. Paperclay with a strong, light effect. Cotton-linter paper. Hot water. Clay slip. Makes an "oatmeal mush." Hard to believe it can be turned into slabs of something beautiful, crystal.

Merle Zirkle creates surprises, mixing unexpected elements with clay. Five-foot-tall "wall climbers": a combination of redwood and clay. "Mortars": clay molded into soft forms with rounded bottoms and perched on PVC pipe. Like an egg on a pedestal, they defy gravity.

Then she breaks away from the soft forms into crystal-shaped forms of slab and molded clay made by hand. Strong hands, formed into a circular shape after years of throwing pots on the wheel.

Merle's lifework is best described by stringing words together with hyphens: scholar-teacher, artist-teacher, mother-artist. Balancing the hyphens presents a lifetime of challenges. "It's a balancing act trying to get in everything you want to do, but teaching still gives you more flexibility for art than a nine-to-five job would." Self-discipline.

Merle's an organizer. She has to be. Time management gurus could learn a thing or two from her. There's the course management. Then she has to record and document her own pieces for shows. Firing a kiln eats hours out of a day. Cleaning up after working with clay takes time, too. "There's a lot of fussy work in art. People think it just happens."

A meticulous worker, Merle keeps a clean shop. Her basement studio is filled with the tools of her art. Dry clay. Wet clay. Color samples. Finished pots. Sculpture. Works in progress: a communion cup for her church. Drawings. Brown paper packages filled with glazing chemicals. Rolling pins. Jars filled with the thick goo she calls underglaze. Big tools: sanders and drills and hacksaws and planes. A firing kiln right next to the washer and dryer.

She's in control. But she knows when to let go, to make way for extraordinary outcomes. "You do what you can to prepare, but the kiln takes over. It's unknown, unpredictable."

A visiting artist at the University of Mississippi in the 1950s impressed Merle, gave her the idea to concentrate in ceramics as a graduate student. Her interests were broad, though. In the early years of her career, she specialized in jewelry making.

"I did jewelry for years and years because I didn't have good personal studio space for clay." Her jewelry won awards. She sold a lot. Many women in Grinnell still don original Zirkles.

Then she was widowed.

She had come to Iowa in the 1960s to teach art and start a craft program at a tiny liberal arts college with her husband Glenn. Like the sixties, they were radical—among the first faculty members in the country to be hired under a shared contract. When he died in 1986, she took over his classes—the sculpture program—at the college.

The class ignited buried instincts. She found herself merging the concepts of sculpture and ceramics. She flowed into a new artistic role: sculptor-ceramist. Her recent productions make evocative statements about humanity, relationships, nature.

The new millennium will manifest another shift in Merle's life. She'll retire from teaching and yield to the genesis of artistic synthesis. Research. Creation. Ritual. Art. It takes time. "I want people to want to live with my artwork."

ᕓ *Denise Lamphier*

Word Portraits

In *Portraits of Iowa Women Artists*, you will find written as well as photographic portraits. Art does not need language in its creation or expression except when the medium is language itself. The essays in this book are art, sharing space with the visual portraits. The word portraits employ language in an effort to reveal creative impulses and motivations, to reveal how and where art is conceived and made. The material of these essays was gleaned through information exchange and formed in the writer's imagination. The essay does not need biographical facts though some may be presented, and it does not aspire to interpret or explain the artist or her work. The essays are constructed using the medium of words, the currency of daily communication and commerce but also of art, just as the artist employs the materials, the colors, the forms of the everyday in her creations. The word portraits are inspired and informed by a particular woman in a particular space, and written with the hope that each contains a truth which allows the reader an expansion of understanding of the creative process, art, and self. These varied forms of art are gathered and presented as a gift, a model of collaboration and celebration.

Paddy Blackman

Katie Kiley

The flutes and pipes lilt a piercing melody above the drums and tambourines chanting the rhythm of a Celtic song. "Don't you just love this?" asks Katie Kiley, turning up the volume. The energy of the music seems to enter her body, and even when the song ends, she keeps moving to its beat. She rises from her chair again and again, standing to gesture or to retrieve a book or piece of art that enlarges the conversation.

Creating art is hard work. An artist needs staying power. Katie has learned that she often "knows one part of a work, but must really struggle with another part." She often generates art from destruction. The "Wrapped Head" series was born when she drew on the remains of a lithograph that failed. The original image slipped off the stone while she washed it with water. "It floated away like a ghost."

Loss informs her art. "Brave Mary" is a series of paintings inspired by two friends who share a name, and personal battles with illness and fate. "But my art is not only about angst. It is also about beauty, beauty as truth." Katie searches for beauty in images that she revisits, images that cannot be exhausted, mythic forms such as trees and humans. A finished piece is usually the result of the "meandering discovery" of the process, but some pieces are fully envisioned before the brush touches canvas. This is how it was with "Guardian of the Body," a painting which came to her as a verbal description in a dream, and which she translated into images.

Her easel stands by the windows in the dining room of the house she shares with her husband and two daughters. She is working on a 24-by-36-inch copper plate, the reversed images beginning to emerge. The dining table is covered with drawings in progress, etching tools, scrapers, scribes, and rags to wipe the plate. Her art hangs on the walls. A tall upright piano laden with framed family photos claims the room as both studio and family space.

Katie left her job as a successful artist in advertising. She is mindful of working as an artist who is also a woman. Her work was rejected by a gallery customer because it was done by a woman. Kiley discovered that she too had learned to undervalue women's art when she was studying in Italy. She encountered a painting in a museum which captivated her attention and drew her to examine the artist's signature. "'Oh, a woman,' I thought disappointedly." Confused by her own reaction, she admits the cultural forces that have pushed on us all. "If I thought that, and I am her, then what can we expect of others?"

Katie acknowledges the injustice and pain she encounters by integrating them into her work. Sometimes the painful truth is the beauty, and other times the beauty of proportion and design is the truth Kiley seeks.

❧ *Paddy Blackman*

Mary Merkel-Hess

Mary Merkel-Hess invites your imagination to sail on a calm sea of grasses in a soft and luminous world. "I want to create tranquility with my art," she says. "I don't want to challenge you but rather to offer a place of rest from the noisy, frantic pace of everyday living." She fashions symmetrical baskets with translucent papers of beige and off-white.

Mary worked first in metalsmithing, creating organically-folded bowls. Wanting vessels larger than metal allowed, she experimented with paper cord. Then, when she and her children were making papier maché, Mary began to develop her own method of constructing paper baskets using small chunks of paper wet with methyl cellulose. Others responded to her work, and she liked the speed of the process. Sometimes handpainted in various intensities of a single hue, her baskets suggest grasses, seed pods, or waving reeds, images invoking her love of landscape.

Mary studied papermaking with Tim Barrett, director of the University of Iowa Center for the Book, who is regarded as the best papermaker in the country. During that time, she adapted her technique for lantern baskets from Japanese traditions. Her first lantern baskets were formed around foam-core molds she collapsed and removed in the traditional way when the paper had dried. Now she leaves the mold where it is, a beautiful structure visible through the translucent *gampi* paper.

The quest for perfect peace is expressed in Mary's calm demeanor and in the pale light of her studio. Beyond the doors is a lush garden tended by her husband. In the room where Mary dips small pieces of paper into a deep bucket of refined wallpaper paste, a painting of St. Dominic hangs on the wall, his index finger across his lips. "I like to remind myself to be still, to leave the world behind when I come into my studio."

A portrait of the Italian Renaissance artist Perugino also hangs nearby. "His art was very popular and then very unpopular. The life of art has always had its vagaries," Mary says. Art as lived by Mary Merkel-Hess revolves around the primordial vessel form, connected both to craft and to daily life. Although the function of baskets has changed with time, we still hunger for the form. Mary's work continues to offer us moments of golden peace.

୬ *Paddy Blackman*

Margaret Whiting

Margaret Whiting makes books, but they aren't exactly about words. When her books include words, they are usually someone else's, cut out of one context and pasted into another. She buys books by the pound and the dozen, at flea markets and withdrawn library sales, estate auctions and thrift shops. She takes stuff apart in her studio, a conceptual editing room where the physical fragments of many different kinds of things become pieces in a creative puzzle she would rather play with than solve.

"We turn to books for knowledge, wisdom, and truth." Her art claims that books are not static, that ideas are alive. One altered book retains the original's embossed hardcover but has new innards. An incomplete encyclopedia set is reborn in her restored yet abridged version. Her edition teases with our expectations of the weighty world of knowledge. No need to sit down; we can hold any one of the seventy-two volumes in our hands. Margaret's encyclopedia about evolution also comments on our destruction of nature's wholeness in both the content and form of each book. The sequential pages are independent of each other, yet interdependent. "If you pulled out one page, the book wouldn't be complete."

A shell mounted atop another one of her altered books honors natural beauty, and suggests we consider the wisdom or truth bound into the shell. The piece resembles a bonsai of ideas, or an oceanic tree that depends for its life on what it can filter or absorb. A book box contains red pine bark sheets. To her, books can be anything that opens, like a geode, or a fossil fish imprinted on two halves of a smoothed sandstone. Looking for things is as important to her as finding them. "It can change my way of thinking," she explains of discovering just the right artifact.

Margaret thrills to nature's abundance. "See how the brain is like the Mississippi River," she says, leafing through her *Field Guide*, one of many books which reveal her appreciation for the cornucopia of similarities between organic forms. Transparent overlays help us find our way among the swirling river channels and miles of gray matter.

She worked for ten years as a medical technologist in hospital laboratories, and practiced weaving and papermaking before she settled on the book arts. "With books, I can express something more specific than I could with weaving. This fits me much better." She moves with ease between precision and playfulness, so different from threading a loom and planning the design in advance. "Now I can work on something, and rework it. I can rip it in half. If I'm not happy, then I'll paint on it. If I'm not satisfied yet, I'll add a fossil. I can keep on working until it feels right."

In an "Environmental Self-Portrait" assembled in a flat picture frame, representations of the river and the brain support a topography made from sawn magazines. Viewers can literally read her issues, tokens from a subscriber to the arts and sciences. Shells represent her two daughters. "My husband and I are these two old fossils," she jokes. By juxtaposing images that we ordinarily think of as separate, she asks us to "read the texture, not the text," the poetry of forms.

இ Marianne Abel

Maureen Seamonds

"**W**inter Dance: Primal Wind." "Winter Spirit Behind Black Veils." These figurative stoneware sculptures by Maureen Seamonds emerge from the kiln in her Produce Station Pottery in downtown Webster City, just a block away from the town's grain elevator and a Hardee's. Maureen stakes her claim for coexistence. "Shadows of September Being." "Blue Spirit Wearing Summer's Veil." She has a subversive knack for accepting things as they are because that's her opening to make things as she would like them to be.

People told her she should be an artist when she grew up. "I was the kind of kid who's always drawing." Her family was supportively neutral. "Nobody asked the practical side of it. They had no way to make it a reality but they didn't create a roadblock." She associates the aroma of oil paint with her Grandpa Kennedy who was famous for his paintings of corn. "Everyone stood back from it and said he paints in the afternoon," she recalls. "His afternoon was respected."

She found it impossible to keep a studio at home with three young children, so she bought the Produce Station building with two women artists in 1985. In 1997, she established a second studio at her family's cabin on Lake Cornelia. Add full-time teaching at Iowa Central Community College in Fort Dodge, and her schedule is a blur. "I used to spend a lot of time organizing and simplifying but actually it really works OK when it's complex and chaotic.

"I set tremendous challenges with every new piece. For me, that's part of the artwork itself, that's part of the mountain—not doing the same thing you've already accomplished." She also feels that her rural setting isolates her from technical resources and public understanding of artistic pursuits. "I find the hardest thing is how do you get taken seriously. Sometimes I feel like I'm their entertainment.

"Most of my real frustrations are not with ideas," Maureen says, "but how to make things work." When she stumbles on a solution, it's usually a reversal of a standard process. She applies conventional underglazes over other glazes, as if she hadn't read the labels. "I just can't put something on straight. It's hard to leave things," she laughs. "Mastering the surface, getting the right color relationship that you wanted when you put the glaze on, is a continual war. The colors are 'true' to what they say, but it's never enough for an artist. I don't know if I'll live long enough to make enough mistakes to learn to do it right."

She inches clay slabs upward, the way gods might have shaped humans by trial and error, knowing that a flaming kiln waits. The undulating surfaces are filigreed with rhythmic calligraphic marks in colored wax pencils. The massive gentle form contrasting with the mesmerizing surface depth creates a sensual trance—in focus, volume, out of focus, weight, foreground, vertical, background, subject, texture, object, color, horizontal.

"I like to think of the human form in the context of landscape. I think a lot about the quality of human gesture—the lean of a shoulder, press of thigh or gaze, directional quality and movement," Maureen comments. "Not what the body looks like, but the breath of life. That simplest gesture is what I'm looking for." "Autumn Whisper: Fireflies Dance." "Spirit of the River Dawn."

↳ *Marianne Abel*

Bonnie Koloc

Winter isn't just a metaphor in Bonnie Koloc's songs. Born and raised in Waterloo, she knows weather, and how different blue skies can be. She warms like a gospel singer to the shock and salvation of true romance, as if the other lush seasons can't atone for abandonment. "Do you remember wintertime? Do you remember ice and snow?" she sings on *With You on My Side*, her ninth album. "Do you remember loneliness? Love makes it seem so long ago."

Someone invented the alto sax to mimic a voice like hers. Companionship and pleasure grate against her wail of yearning for connections that cannot be, or cannot survive, or have already died. "If there is one theme in all my work, it's that life is hard. You find a way to get through it, and come out better for it." Her strongest faith is in humor, without which she says she'd be lost. Her soulmates are dogs. When she imagines heaven, it's "where artists and good dogs go."

Bonnie started singing when she was three years old. In college she turned to drama, then to art, then she tried music to make a living. She dropped out at twenty-three to board the Illinois Central at midnight in Waterloo, headed for a dawn in Chicago that arrived the next day. It's a dream of success she keeps trying to reach, as elusive and irritating as a spring wind. Her albums and performances, from Broadway to the Troubadour, tally many years in Nashville, New York City, and her spiritual hometown, Chicago.

She shelters her privacy in a hideout—an apartment here, an old house not far from the river there, or it might be an evening or morning somewhere in the middle that's memorialized in a chorus or a lullaby. In between engagements, she returns to marked territory, an acreage on a ridgetop in northeast Iowa where the walls are block-printed with her stamps. Curtains filter light through her patterns. Furniture gleams with her paints. At home, she creates fiber works, drawings, prints, songs, gardens, and shrines.

"Tales from Trashmania," her current multi-media production, combines her favorite forms into a one-person show that toys with her classic themes. Bonnie conjures the circus to exaggerate how we explore what we're born to do. "Everyone has a talent: it's a challenge to use it well." The Trashmanians are "the last survivors of a language and culture of nomads who all use their gifts." This outrageous fantasy fictionalizes her Bohemian ancestors interacting with animals in a musical scale hopscotch that would enchant any scat singer.

She thrives on contrast. Part of life is as tacky as the 3-D Jesuses she collects from thrift shops, the ones in gilt frames with their own museum lights, or as wacky as her rhymes about cats or chickens. No matter what form Bonnie picks up, she's always looking for that line—through a melody, to a destination, onto the blank page. She's become the artist she always wanted to be. Not as elegant as she dreamed, not as famous as she hoped, but alive, working through it, and some nights, much to her grateful surprise, feeling loved and blessed.

Marianne Abel

Ingrid Bogdanowicz

Shouldering her oversized gym bag, Ingrid breezes between the glass doors of the Wiese Art Building. When she catches sight of us her eyes shine. We follow her down the dim tunnel of cement steps to the basement. Pushing open the industrial-height door, she ushers us into the cavernous studio/classroom. A wall of windows frames the Mississippi River valley below Museum Hill. Inside, the press holds center stage. Raw materials and tools of printmaking spill out of cabinets and across countertops.

The concrete floors show blots and splashes of color. A bulletin board is alive with paintings, drawings, and Ingrid's colorful monoprints and powerfully detailed black-and-white etchings.

Seating ourselves on a workbench, we listen to Ingrid's odyssey in art from her childhood in Germany to her place in the Quad Cities artists' community. She speaks quietly, her r's full and soft.

"I never really knew my father. He was a casualty of World War II. My mother was talented in art and crafts. She and my teachers encouraged me. I was always being asked to draw for people. They said I had a talent for life drawing.

"There were many opportunities for art in German schools. I loved it. I worked on every project until I succeeded." She laughs lightly. "Now I would do art even if no one appreciated it. I guess it's in my genes. I have to do some art every day.

"Wherever I have lived—and the wife of an American military man can move a lot—I've sought out the creative community, taking lessons, producing paintings, drawings, prints. I'm a people-person, and while I spend much time dreaming and planning in my mind, I enjoy not only teaching but working in the company of others."

ᔆ *Kay Kehoe and Harriet Harmelink*

Harriet Harmelink

Rowen Schussheim-Anderson

"There was a ruddiness everywhere in the landscape," recalls Rowen of her mideighties trip to the Andes. Clay-red rooftops, scalloped and thick. Brown faces, cheeks naturally and indelibly red from the sun and mountain air. Green patchwork countryside under continuous cultivation. Such colors have become the stuff of Rowen's work. Sturdy sisal, dyed in the reds and browns of the Andes, she has woven into the designs and textures from this indelible part of her experience.

"In a sense I am attempting to 'paint' with fiber," says Rowen. "Surface quality and temperature are important ingredients. Hot and cool lines of color placed side-by-side vibrate, shock, and dance. Matisse, Henri Moore, Magdalena Abakanowicz, Paul Klee, and kindergartners have all influenced me."

Even daughter Sydney was once made a co-creator. On a day when Rowen left her partial design for a weaving on the kitchen counter, the purple construction paper and magic marker were irresistible. Rowen's dense thicket of vertical strokes with half-spirals here and there like exploration were answered with four firm statements from Sydney. Two long border lines confined the left. On the right, one longer line reached up to its own curled top. And in the middle, a decisive horizontal line both divided and connected what was above and what was below. Rowen could see that her child was offering to take part in the design. She

worked out the purple-on-purple on the loom. The result was christened "Child's Offering."

Rowen's own offering, her legacy to children as well as adults, includes founding and directing Kaleidoscope, the community art program at Augustana College in Rock Island, Illinois. And just across the Mississippi River in Iowa, Rowen's "Line Dance" holds pride of place at the circulation station of the Bettendorf Public Library and Information Center. Reminiscent of "Child's Offering," a dense thicket of Rowen's trademark "hot and cool" colors in vertical strokes nod and bend

toward one another in their dance across the large alcove wall. Like tall, thick blades of bright grass, or the fanned leaves of a wide-spined book, "Line Dance" inhabits and infuses the lively communal landscape with a vibrancy of its own.

꩜ *Carol Lauhon*

Judith Miller

Life in the West is permeated by one fact: the inescapable presence of rock. For Judy Miller, growing up near Phoenix meant the red-orange palette of Arizona canyons, brilliant sunsets beyond the Superstition Mountains, and the sparkling mineral hardpan, "caliche," that paves the desert floor. And above all, the endlessly arching turquoise sky whose light sharpens substance and shadows alike.

Despite the soft gray Iowa light, Judy manages to breathe the light and substance of the Southwest into her sculpture. Even the most neutral glaze on her smaller pieces imparts a translucence born of clear air and brilliant light. One studio wall is occupied by a full-scale piece that evokes the niches and crags of the road-cut rock face. Judy says her love for sculpture grew from her fascination with light playing off landscape. "You can see color, even see *through* color, wherever you turn in the Southwest. Even though I was trained in printmaking, I was lured to sculpture by texture and strength. And I love the fact that three-dimensional work doesn't depend on the illusion of one plane existing in front of another."

Although this sculptural honesty intrigues Judy, her work contains some of its own illusions and surprises. For all its monumental, weighty appearance, the sculpture on her studio wall is constructed of thin sheets of high-fired porcelain. Despite its rugged lithic appearance, the porcelain has a soft, fine-toothed surface. And although the piece seems to display all the quirks of nature and coincidences of Fate, its creation was a complex, well-considered process. "Like much in nature, this piece looks haphazard. But to create breaks and cracks in rock that really look naturalistic demands considerable forethought and an understanding of how both nature and these particular artistic materials work."

Judy's work relates to the natural world, and she believes that throughout their evolution, humans have retained an important need to respond to nature in an aesthetic sense. "I'm drawn to the nonsymmetrical and subtle, the tactile and seductive. We have become experts at contriving new forms, even new life forms. But if they don't at least appear to come from nature, they don't appeal to us, at least for long. I want my art to link us with the natural world, to bridge the gap between what once was and what is, between our natural senses and our constructed life."

The world Judy constructs includes porcelain lamps whose organic shapes glow from the light within and porcelain "puppets" depicting gently smiling old women with walking sticks. She delights in the ragged edges of torn clay that she purposefully exposes, and the shattered pieces of broken porcelain that she incorporates into other artworks.

She says that we've become accustomed to thinking of things that are torn or broken or cut-through as ugly, destroyed. "But I think our value judgments often are more a matter of focus than a perception of reality. It's easy to think a road-cut is ugly. But if we pause to look carefully, it can reveal beautiful shapes, textures, and colors.

"The cut-through isn't aesthetic until we really focus and examine it. Nature, like art, is a matter of attention."

∞ *Jean Florman*

Nancy Briggs

Just as fire consumed the pieces of Nancy Briggs' life more than twenty years ago, today she consumes fact, myth, and legend to create sculptures of women who wrestle with the circumstances of their lives to gain control. Nancy's efforts to rein in her own life are evident in her art, emotionally jarring pieces of women bursting from flaming houses, crematoriums, and volcanoes. She controls fire by raku firing her sculptures, coaxing colors from the clay and glazes.

"I was a very young woman when my house burned down around me. I lost everything—even my cat for a while. I was singed, but I survived."

It's a constant message of her art, that even in difficult times, women are survivors, and they triumph. She was the model for the sculpture of the woman, dressed in a nightgown, bursting through the roof of the burning house.

"I used a mirror to capture the grimace and terror from my own face, and the claw-clenched hands grasping for fresh air."

Destruction was evident in "Phalanx: 'We Have Met the Enemy and He is Us,'" a collection of eighteen figures depicting warriors from past and present. Each of the figures had a baby face and wore period warrior clothing.

"'Phalanx' was an anti-war memorial. I wanted people to see that we nurture our children, and then we surrender them to war later. I used a doll mold to create the figures' baby faces, and the bottoms of the sculptures resembled shell casings. I inscribed each of the figures with a quote," she says.

One set of figures was a Vietnamese soldier, with "Born in North Vietnam, died in South Vietnam" on the casing. The other was an American soldier, inscribed with "To Charlie, With Love."

"The war in Vietnam wasn't the first time weapons included written statements or threats. It's probably been done since the first human picked up a rock to hurl it in anger at another," Nancy says. The Phalanx, now with separate collectors, received special recognition at the 1990 Iowa Artist Show at the Des Moines Art Center.

Today, Briggs is inspired by the lives of famous and infamous women. Through a series of fifteen sculptures, she is bringing the stories of these women to life. "Joan of Arc, who will be included, inspired the title, 'Women Who Dare: We Will Strike With Great Thunder and We Shall See Who Has Their Rights.'" .

The series will include Boadicia, the warrior queen of the Celts who defended her village from the Romans who invaded Britain. "Boadicia battled the Roman soldiers, who had raped and pillaged and burned their way through the Celts' villages," she says.

The women, who will be dressed in appropriate clothing and accouterments made of clay and decorated with glazes, will rise from triangular bases, and all fifteen will be displayed in a triangular formation. Each will be inscribed with a quote attributed to the woman.

"The quote for Boadicia is 'Pray for victory against men, both insolent and unjust.' One thing these women all have in common is that they intrigue me. Mata Hari, who will be included in the work, is not particularly admirable, but she was very interesting," Nancy says. The collection will be finished during the spring of 1998.

As she has expanded the list of women from admirable to interesting, Nancy has expanded her own experience, teaching children and adults sculpting at the Des Moines Art Center.

"If you want to be the center of attention, where they have to listen to you, teach! And teach those who really want to learn. I find teaching very rewarding, and I learn from my students, too. The clay allows so many children to communicate, even if all they do is poke indentations into the clay," Nancy says.

Through the Iowa Yucatan Partners cultural exchange program, Nancy taught an adult ceramics class at the Museo Artes Contemperano Ateneo Yucatan. Her husband, Peter Stephano, accompanied her on the trip to Mexico. "We toured the ruins of Yucatan. I've come back with more ideas for new sculptures, and the consuming desire to finish projects!"

Dawn Bowman

The Queen Is in the Parlor, 1995.
welded steel armature and neckties
28"H x 34"W x 13"D

Annin, Marilyn
Ames, Iowa
Born: 1938, Madison, Wisconsin
Sculptor

Education: B.S., University of Wisconsin–Madison

Selected solo exhibitions:
> 1997 "Garments as Metaphor," Witter Gallery, Storm Lake, Iowa
> 1989 "Games/Garments," Grinnell Community Art Gallery, Grinnell, Iowa
> 1980 Minnesota Governor's Residence, St. Paul, Minnesota

A Place in Mind, 1997
acrylic and metallic colored pencil
15¼" x 22½"

Banks-Craighead, Verna
Davenport, Iowa
Born: 1930, Philadelphia, Pennsylvania
Mixed media artist

Education: Art workshops and seminars

Selected exhibitions:
> 1997 "Showing Off," Central Iowa Women's Caucus for the Arts, Cedar Rapids Museum of Art, Cedar Rapids, Iowa
> 1997 Fort Madison Art Center, Fort Madison, Iowa Solo exhibition
> 1993 Clinton Art Center, Clinton, Iowa Two-person exhibition

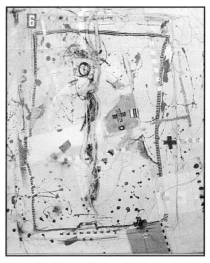

Cross My Heart/Hope to Die I, 1995.
mixed media
43" x 54"

Behrens, Mary Snyder
Dysart, Iowa
Born: 1957, Milwaukee, Wisconsin
Painter/mixed media artist

Education: B.F.A., University of Wisconsin–Madison

Selected exhibitions:
> 1997 "Fantastic Fibers," Yeiser Art Center, Paducah, Kentucky
> 1997 "Red Hot Art," Campbell/Steele Gallery Marion, Iowa
> 1993 "Clothing as Human Expression," Johnson County Art Center, Iowa City, Iowa

Mother/Art Journeys, 1994.
functional jacket with pockets containing
handmade booklets
Sized to be worn

Bennett, Astrid Hilger
Iowa City, Iowa
Born: 1953, Remscheid, Germany
Fiber artist

Education: B.F.A., Indiana University

Selected exhibitions:
      1996 Luther College, Decorah, Iowa
            Solo exhibition
      1996 "Clay and Fiber Invitational," Kirkwood Community
            College, Cedar Rapids, Iowa
      1994 Earlham College, Richmond, Indiana
            Solo exhibition

Winter, Iowa City, 1970.
intaglio print
6" x 10"

Bergmann, Leola
Iowa City, Iowa
Born: 1912, South Dakota
Printmaker

Education: Ph.D, University of Iowa

Selected solo exhibitions:
      1994 Iowa Artisans Gallery, Iowa City, Iowa
      1987 University of Iowa Hospitals and Clinics, Iowa
            City, Iowa
      1986 Kirkwood Community College, Cedar Rapids,
            Iowa

Innocence, from Crisis of the Black Male series, 1989.
charcoal
20" x 24"

Berry, Jean
Des Moines, Iowa
Born: 1938, Okmulgee, Oklahoma
Multimedia artist

Education: B.F.A., Drake University

Selected exhibitions:
      1997 "Middle Passage of Three," Luther College,
            Decorah, Iowa
      1997 Greater Des Moines Exhibition, Heritage Art
            Gallery, Des Moines, Iowa
      1991 "Fourteen Stations of the Cross," Huston Tillitson
            College, Austin, Texas

Dreamer's Voyage, 1997.
watercolor
7½" x 10"

Bieber, Connie
Davenport, Iowa
Born: 1954, Davenport, Iowa
Painter

Education: Study at Marycrest College, University of Iowa

Selected exhibitions:
    1996 "Rock Island Fine Arts Exhibition," Centennial
           Hall Gallery, Augustana College, Rock Island,
           Illinois
    1995 "Bi-State Competitive Art Exhibition," Davenport
           Museum of Art, Davenport, Iowa
    1984 Iowa Watercolor Society, Waterloo, Iowa

Left – *Christina*, 16"H x 10"W x 12"D
Right – *Birdwatcher*, 8"H x 11"W x 17"D
cast concrete

Bloom, Isabel
Davenport, Iowa
Born: 1908, Galveston, Texas
Sculptor

Education: Vogue School of Design
              Chicago Art Institute
              Grant Wood Art Colony

The Last Dance, 1996.
drypoint with engraving
5" x 8"

Bogdanowicz, Ingrid
Davenport, Iowa
Born: 1939, Coburg, Germany
Printmaker, Painter

Education: El Portal Institute for the Fine Arts
              Augustana College
              Davenport Museum of Art

Selected exhibitions:
    1995 "Viva Elvis," Davenport Museum of Art, Davenport,
           Iowa
    1987 "Women at Work," Centennial Hall Gallery,
           Augustana College, Rock Island, Illinois
    1979 Quad City Arts Gallery, Rock Island, Illinois, Solo
           exhibition

Performance in Butterfly Batik Costume, 1980s.

Boyd, Sarah Jane
Davenport, Iowa
Born: 1945, Davenport, Iowa
Multimedia artist

Education: B.A., St. Ambrose University
B.A., Marycrest College

Selected exhibitions:
1997 "Iowa Teachers Exhibit," Iowa City, Iowa
1995 Blue Moon Café and Gallery, Galena, Illinois
1993 "Imaging Quad Cities Women Artists," Davenport Museum of Art, Davenport, Iowa

Without Mercy or Pity, 1995.
ceramic and wire
17"H x 13"W x 15"D

Briggs, Nancy
Des Moines, Iowa
Born: 1953, Waukesha, Wisconsin
Ceramic artist

Education: B.S., University of Wisconsin, Stevens Point

Selected solo exhibitions:
1996 "Clay/Paper/Metal/Fiber," Octagon Center for the Arts, Ames, Iowa
1995 "Iowa Artists," Des Moines Art Center, Des Moines, Iowa
1993 "Women's Voice, Mirror of the Self," Drake University, Des Moines, Iowa

Untitled, 1995.
oil on black printer's paper
44" x 30"

Burns-Knutson, Sharon
Cedar Rapids, Iowa
Born: 1948, Iowa City, Iowa
Painter

Education: B.A., University of Northern Iowa
M.A., M.F.A., University of Iowa

Selected exhibitions:
1998 Olson-Larsen Galleries, Des Moines, Iowa
1990 Lumina Gallery, San Francisco, California
1984 Peter Moller Gallery, Chicago, Illinois

Memory Boards, 1994.
mixed media
33"H x 54"W x 35"D

Connelly, Karin Stevens
Grinnell, Iowa
Born: 1939, Great Falls, Montana
Feminist artist

Education: M.F.A., University of Iowa

Selected exhibitions:
    1997 "Showing Off," Central Iowa Women's Caucus for
        the Arts, Cedar Rapids Museum of Art, Cedar
        Rapids, Iowa
    1995 "The River: The Waste Stream," Grinnell
        Community Center, Grinnell, Iowa
    1995 "Good Girls/Bad Girls," University of Iowa
        Hospitals and Clinics and Women's Resource and
        Action Center, Iowa City, Iowa

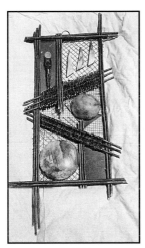

Wall Mural, 1997.
mixed media—clay, willow, copper
20" x 12"

Dennis, Pam
Ogden, Iowa
Born: 1951, Cherry Point, North Carolina
3-D mixed media artist

Education: Des Moines Area Community College

Selected exhibitions:
    1996 Sioux City Arts Center, Sioux City, Iowa
        Solo exhibition
  1991-1996 Iowa Crafts group exhibit, Charles MacNider
        Museum, Mason City, Iowa

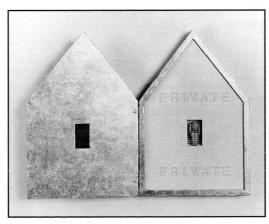

Private Parts, 1996.
metal, glass, silver leaf, fabric, paper, found objects
17½"H x 23"W x 2"D

Ellinwood, Sheryl
Pella, Iowa
Born: 1959, Toledo, Ohio
Sculptor, glass blower

Education: B.F.A., University of Toledo
           M.F.A., Southern Illinois University-Carbondale

Selected exhibitions:
    1997 Buena Vista University, Storm Lake, Iowa
        Solo exhibition
    1996 Vetro Marmo Gallery, Columbus, Ohio
        Solo exhibition
    1996 Kansas City Artists' Coalition, Kansas City, Missouri
        Two-person exhibition

Bird of Paradise, 1993.
whirligig—mixed media
18"H x 24"W x 6"D

Ernst, Colleen

Iowa City, Iowa
Born: 1951, Burlington, Iowa
Painter

Education: B.A., Northwestern University

Selected exhibitions:
      1997 "D.V.I.P. Fine Art Exhibit," Iowa City, Iowa
      1995 "Paintings and Assemblages," Olson-Larsen
            Galleries, West Des Moines, Iowa
            Solo exhibition
      1993 "New Work," University of Iowa Hospitals and
            Clinics, Iowa City, Iowa
            Solo exhibition

Containment/Contentment, 1996.
framed fiber collage
19" x 24"

Friedman, Jan

Iowa City, Iowa
Born: 1959, Carroll, Iowa

Education: B.A., Art Education, University of Iowa
             M.A., Textile Design, University of Iowa

Selected exhibitions:
      1996 Iowa State Bank and Trust Co., Iowa City
      1995 Fiber/Metal, St. Paul, Minnesota
      1984 Yamanashi Prefectural Museum of Art, Kofu,
            Japan

Windows, 1995.
wood, metal, video
8'H x 8'W x 5'D

Gilmor, Jane

Cedar Rapids, Iowa
Born: 1947, Ames, Iowa
Intermedia artist

Education: B.S., Iowa State University
             M.A.T., M.A., M.F.A., University of Iowa

Selected solo exhibitions:
      1997 A.I.R. Gallery, New York, New York
      1994 Bemis Gallery for Contemporary Art, Omaha,
            Nebraska
      1989 NAME Gallery, Chicago, Illinois

The Last Golden Years of Latency, 1996
mixed media installation
8'H x 6'W x 4'D

White Porcelain Pitcher, 1996.
13" x 6"

Transplant, 1995.
charcoal on paper and vellum, gold thread
30" x 22"

Hall, Laurie Elizabeth Talbot
Riverside, Iowa
Born: 1955, Council Bluffs, Iowa
Photographer/installation artist

Education: M.F.A., University of Iowa
Ph.D., University of Iowa

Selected exhibitions:
1997 "You May Never Leave Home," CSPS, Cedar
Rapids, Iowa
Two-person exhibition
1997 "The Magic Silver Show," University of Northern
Iowa, Cedar Falls, Iowa
1996 "The First Eleven Years," Quad City Arts Center,
Rock Island, Illinois
Solo exhibition

Illian, Clary
Ely, Iowa
Born: 1940, Sioux City, Iowa
Potter

Education: B.F.A., University of Iowa
Apprenticeship, The Leach Pottery, England

Selected exhibitions and publications:
1998 *A Potter's Workbook,* University of Iowa Press
1993 "Daily Rituals," Pottery Northwest, Seattle,
Washington
1982 Coe College Art Gallery, Cedar Rapids, Iowa
Solo exhibition

Kames BVM, Louise
Dubuque, Iowa
Born: 1955, Aurora, Illinois
Painter

Education: B.A., Clarke College
M.A., University of Illinois-Urbana
M.F.A., University of Wisconsin-Madison

Selected exhibitions:
1997 Fine Arts Department Gallery, Loyola University,
Chicago, Illinois
1996 Oberpfalzer Kunstlerhaus, Schwandorf, Germany
1996 Cedar Rapids Museum of Art, Cedar Rapids,
Iowa

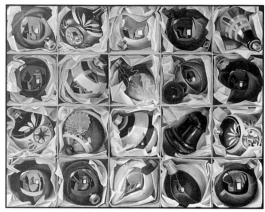

Christmas Ornaments, 1981.
oil on canvas
46¼" x 58¼"

Kerrigan BVM, Helen
Dubuque, Iowa
Born: 1921, Davenport, Iowa
Painter

Education: B.A., Clarke College
M.F.A., Catholic University of America

Selected exhibitions:
1992 "Rock Island Fine Arts Exhibition," Augustana
College, Rock Island, Illinois
1986 Divine Word College, Epworth, Iowa
1985 Old Jail Gallery, Dubuque, Iowa

Repository, 1989-90.
black and white intaglio
36" x 24"

Kiley, Katie
Davenport, Iowa
Born: 1951, Danville, Illinois
Painter/printmaker

Education: B.F.A., St. Ambrose University
M.A., University of Iowa
M.F.A., University of Iowa

Selected exhibitions:
1997 "Flash Point," Quad City Arts Gallery, Rock
Island, Illinois
1997 "Katie Kiley: Paintings, Drawings, and Prints,"
Dartmouth College, Hanover, New Hampshire
1995 "Whiskey Gods and Cold Black Beads," Alfons
Gallery, Milwaukee, Wisconsin

*Adam Offers Eve the Apple (the Dog Knows
the Real Story)*, 1989.
linoleum cut
13" x 10"

Koloc, Bonnie
Northeast Iowa
Born: 1944, Waterloo, Iowa
Multimedia visual artist, singer, songwriter

Education: B.A., University of Northern Iowa

Selected exhibitions:
1996 Lovely Fine Arts, Oakbrook Terrace, Illinois
Solo exhibition
1996 "Cover to Cover: Transformation of the Book,"
Iowa State University, Ames, Iowa
1996 Iowa State Fair, Best of Show for "The Bestiary"

Bat and Pangolin, 1996
gelatin silver print
6½" x 8½"

Macomber, Carol

Cedar Falls, Iowa
Born: 1938, Wilkes-Barre, Pennsylvania
Photographer

Education: B.S., Lawrence College of Wisconsin

Selected exhibitions:
    1996-97 "Iowa Prairie: Selected Views and Voices," Iowa Sesquicentennial touring exhibition
    1996 "Clay Sculpture and Photographs," University of Wisconsin, LaCrosse, Wisconsin
    1995 "Carol Macomber, Photographs," Pacific Grove Art Center, Pacific Grove, California

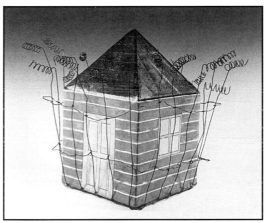

You Can't Have Any More Pieces of My Heart-I, 1995.
mixed media
8½"H x 12"W x 12"D

Martin, Emily

Iowa City, Iowa
Born: 1953, Cedar Rapids, Iowa
Painter, sculptor, book artist

Education: B.F.A., University of Iowa
              M.F.A., University of Iowa

Selected exhibitions:
    1997 "Image and Text," Stephen F. Austin State University, Nacogdoches, Texas
    1996 "Turning the Page," International Book Arts Exhibit, Academy Art Center, Honolulu, Hawaii
    1996 "Oaxaca Print Exchange," Taller de Artes Plasticas/ Galeri Rufino Tamayo, Oaxaca, Mexico

Birch-Rimmed Basket, 1996.
gampi paper, paper board, birch bark
12"H x 7"W x 7"D

Merkel-Hess, Mary

Iowa City, Iowa
Born: 1949, Gilbertville, Iowa
Fiber artist

Education: B.A., Marquette University
              B.F.A., University of Wisconsin-Milwaukee
              M.F.A., University of Iowa

Selected exhibitions:
    1996 "New Works, Mary Merkel-Hess," Brown/Grotta Gallery, Wilton, Connecticut
    1996 "It's More Than a Basket ...," Connell Gallery, Atlanta, Georgia
    1994 "Ceramic and Fiber: A New Generation," Wustum Museum of Fine Arts, Racine, Wisconsin

Ragtime Mama, 1996.
acrylic on canvas
18" x 24"

Shelter
porcelain, acrylics
140"H x 34"W x 18"D

Sprinklers and Bathtime, 1994.
mixed media on paper
50" x 60"

Mesick, Sheila Shumaker

Davenport, Iowa
Born: 1955, Davenport, Iowa
Painter

Education: B.A., St. Ambrose University

Selected exhibitions:

1993 "Imaging Quad Cities Women Artists," Davenport Museum of Art, Davenport, Iowa
1992 "Self-Portraiture in Art," Marycrest College, Davenport, Iowa
1988 "Artists Who Teach," Davenport Museum of Art, Davenport, Iowa

Miller, Judith

Iowa City/Lake Macbride, Iowa
Born: 1940, St. Louis, Missouri
Ceramic sculptor

Education: B.A., Milwaukee Downer College
M.A., Ohio State University
M.F.A., University of Iowa

Selected exhibitions:

1993 Iowa Artisans Gallery, Iowa City, Iowa
1992 Hearst Center for the Arts, Cedar Falls, Iowa
1991 Arbor Gallery, Iowa City, Iowa
Solo exhibition

Morales, Concetta

Des Moines, Iowa
Born: 1960, Brooklyn, New York
Painter/muralist

Education: B.S., Skidmore College
M.F.A., School of the Art Institute of Chicago

Selected exhibitions:

1994-97 "Land of the Fragile Giants," Brunnier Museum, Iowa State University, Ames, Iowa
1994 University of LaCrosse, LaCrosse, Wisconsin
Solo exhibition
1991 "Women's Work," Iowa Sister States Sponsored Show, Stavropol, Russia

St. Lucy, 1994.
oil on panel
14" x 12"

Moongates 3: Starry Nights, 1997.
clay, underglaze paint
42"H x 28"W x 12"D

Birth and Death of a World Series: Cradle/Casket, 1988.
woven branches, gampi, acrylic paint, graphite,
monofilament, paper rush
50"H x 20"W x 12"D

Artists' Biographies and Sample Artworks

Quinn, Kristin
Davenport, Iowa
Born: 1962, Washington, D.C.
Painter

Education: B.F.A., Tyler School of Art
M.F.A., Indiana University

Selected exhibitions:
1994 Quad City Arts, Rock Island, Illinois
Two-person exhibition
1994 Project Art, University of Iowa Hospitals and
Clinics, Iowa City, Iowa
Solo exhibition
1993 "Iowa Artists," Des Moines Art Center, Des
Moines, Iowa

Seamonds, Maureen
Webster City, Iowa
Born: 1945, Miami, Florida
Sculptor, clay

Education: B.A., Iowa State University
M.A., Iowa State University
M.F.A., University of Iowa

Selected exhibitions:
1996 "New Work: Engaging the Interior," Blanden Art
Museum, Fort Dodge, Iowa
1995 "Celebrate Her Vision," University of Illinois,
Champaign, Illinois
1994 "Art Show Seven," Hearst Center for the Arts, Cedar
Falls, Iowa

Schedl, Naomi
Iowa City, Iowa
Born: 1920, Capetown, South Africa
Mixed media artist

Education: M.F.A., Yale University
Post-graduate work, American University, University of
Iowa

Selected exhibitions:
1995 "The River: Seen, Unseen and the Waste Stream,"
Katherine Nash Gallery, University of Minnesota
1989 "Birth and Death of a World," Artimesia Gallery,
Chicago, Illinois
1988 University of Iowa Art Museum, Iowa City, Iowa

Post Meridian, 1992.
mixed media fabric
15" x 20"

Schussheim-Anderson, Rowen

Davenport, Iowa
Born: 1953, Cleveland, Ohio
Fiber artist

Education: B.F.A., School for American Crafts, Rochester Institute of
Technology
M.F.A., Arizona State University

Selected exhibitions:
1993 "Common Threads," Performing Arts Gallery,
Davenport, Iowa
1992 "Peruvian Impressions: Rowen Schussheim-
Anderson Tapestries," Quad City Arts Gallery,
Rock Island, Illinois
1981 "Tapestries in Two and Three Dimensions,"
Yuma Art Center, Yuma, Arizona

Awkward Peeping, 1995.
artist book
8"H x 4"W x 4"D

Soppe, Joan

Cedar Rapids, Iowa
Born: 1968, Cedar Rapids, Iowa
Book artist

Education: B.F.A., Clarke College
M.A., M.F.A., University of Iowa

Selected solo exhibitions:
1997 "Artist's Books," Wakeley Gallery, Illinois
Wesleyan University, Bloomington, Illinois
1996 "Required Reading," Iowa Gallery, Cedar Rapids
Museum of Art, Cedar Rapids, Iowa
1990 "Birth of an Image," Quigley Gallery, Clarke
College, Dubuque, Iowa

Run Without Resting, 1990.
chine collé etching
5" x 6"

Steele, Priscilla

Marion, Iowa
Born: 1951, Camp LeJeune, North Carolina
Printmaker

Education: B.A., St. Lawrence University
M.A., M.F.A., University of Iowa

Selected solo exhibitions:
1993 Coe College, Cedar Rapids, Iowa
1992 "Iowa Print Group," Hamburg, Germany
1986 Creighton University, Omaha, Nebraska

Self-Portrait: My Stepfather's Den, 1988.
gelatin silver print
7" x 10"

Steinbach, Imogene "Robbie"

Bettendorf, Iowa
Born: 1948, Belle Plaine, Iowa
Photographer

Education: B.A., University of Northern Iowa
M.A., M.F.A., University of Iowa

Selected exhibitions:
1997 "You May Never Leave Home," CSPS, Cedar
Rapids, Iowa
Two-person exhibition
1995 "Wishing You Were Home, Darling," Quad City
Arts, Rock Island, Illinois
Solo exhibition
1993 "Imaging Quad Cities Women Artists," Davenport
Museum of Art, Davenport, Iowa

Architectural Detailings at Random, 1997.
artist-made book, web site
680 x 440 pixels

Stensaas, Starla

Logan, Iowa
Born: 1956, Madison, South Dakota
Book artist

Education: B.A., Eastern Illinois University
M.A., Eastern Illinois University
M.F.A., University of Wisconsin-Milwaukee

Selected exhibitions:
1995 SIGGRAPH '95 Art Gallery, Los Angeles, California
1993 "Starla Stensaas, Artist Made Books," Mount
Angel Abbey Library Rare Book Room, Mount
Angel, Oregon
1987 "Women's Autobiographical Artists' Books,"
University of Wisconsin-Milwaukee   Art
Museum, Milwaukee, Wisconsin

An Album for Your Imagination's Memory, 1993.
mixed media artist book
7¼"H x 11¼"W x 1"D

Stepanek, Sally

Brooklyn, New York
Born: 1960, Chicago, Illinois
Mixed media artist and writer

Education: B.A., Yale University
M.F.A., University of Iowa Writers' Workshop

Selected exhibitions and publications:
Various artist books and public art installations
Arts writer and editor, *Literární Noviny*, Prague, Czech
Republic
Arts writer and editor, *Tractor: A Quarterly Magazine of
Iowa Arts and Culture*, Cedar Rapids, Iowa

Opening Theme, 1994.
oil
36" x 24"

Sunday, Ben, a.k.a. Mildred Dain
Davenport, Iowa
Born: 1926, Davenport, Iowa
Painter

Education: Self-taught, workshops

Selected exhibitions:
       1991   Harlequin Award, Riverssance Arts Festival,
                  Davenport, Iowa
       1960's Taught Ben Sunday Art School
       1950's Conceived and organized Studio 15 Gallery,
                  Davenport, Iowa

Stella's Blue Sky Diner, 1995.
pastel
40" x 60"

Wagener, Ellen
DeWitt, Iowa
Born: 1964, DeWitt, Iowa
Painter

Education: B.A., Corcoran School of Art

Selected solo exhibitions:
       1997 "New Pastels," Olson-Larsen Galleries, West Des
                  Moines, Iowa
       1996 "Not Quite Utopia," Quad City Arts Gallery, Rock
                  Island, Illinois
       1994 John Canon Gallery, Washington, D.C.

Fallen Sable #Two, 1990.
clay, low fired, smoked
80"L x 56"W x 11"D

Ward, Nina de Creeft
Cedar Falls, Iowa
Born: 1933, New York, New York
Sculptor

Education: B.A., Scripps College
               M.F.A., Claremont Graduate School

Selected solo exhibitions:
       1997 "Rhino/Blaauwbock Project," Waterloo Museum of
                  Art, Waterloo, Iowa
       1995 "Anxious Moments," Pacific Grove Art Center,
                  Pacific Grove, California
       1988 "Fragments and Conversations," Leedy Voulkos
                  Gallery, Kansas City, Kansas

Snapshot: Redfish, Idaho, 1995.
acrylic on paper
23" x 30"

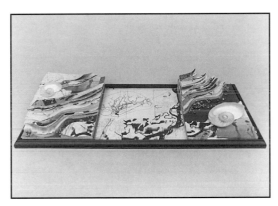

Geology, 1996.
artist book
28"L x 12"W x 3"D

Six from "Portraits of Dubuque," 1992.
pastel
30" x 20" each

Wegman, Marcia
Iowa City, Iowa
Born: 1935, Washington, D.C.
Painter, mixed media

Education: B.F.A., Miami University
M.F.A., University of Iowa

Selected exhibitions:
1996 Nina Liu and Friends Gallery, Charleston, South Carolina
Solo exhibition
1996 Senior Center, Iowa City, Iowa
Solo exhibition
1996 Cedar Rapids Museum of Art, Cedar Rapids, Iowa

Whiting, Margaret
Iowa City, Iowa
Born: 1954, Virginia, Minnesota
Multimedia book artist

Education: B.S., University of Minnesota

Selected exhibitions:
1996-97 "Iowa Prairie: Selected Views and Voices," Iowa Sesquicentennial touring exhibition
1996 "Turning the Page," International Book Arts Exhibition, Academy Art Center, Honolulu, Hawaii
1996 "Merged Realities, A Synthesis of Art and Science," Central Arts Collective, Tucson, Arizona

Woodward, Tilly
Pella, Iowa
Born: 1957, Monticello, Illinois
Visual artist

Education: B.A., Kansas City Art Institute
M.F.A., University of Kansas

Selected solo exhibitions:
1997 Blanden Art Museum, Fort Dodge, Iowa
1992 Dubuque Museum of Art, Dubuque, Iowa
1987 Addison Gallery of American Art, Phillips Academy, Andover, Massachusetts

Sotoportego de la Bissa, 1994.
engraving
9" x 8"

The River: Time Is a River Without Banks, 1986.
cast iron; view of installation
33' x 26½'

Holbrook Greenhouse, 1996.
intaglio
18" x 15"

Worthen, Amy

Des Moines, Iowa
Born: 1946, New York, New York
Printmaker

Education: B.A., Smith College
            M.A., University of Iowa

Selected solo exhibitions:
    1996 Scuola Internazionale di Grafica, Venice, Italy
    1992 Ecole Régionale Des Beaux-Arts, Saint-Étienne,
          France
    1990 Grinnell College, Grinnell, Iowa

Wyrick, Shirley

Iowa City, Iowa
Born: Des Moines, Iowa
Sculptor

Education: B.A., University of Iowa
            M.A., M.F.A., University of Iowa

Selected solo exhibitions:
    1993 Muscatine Art Center, Muscatine, Iowa
    1992 "Listening to the River," University of Iowa Thea-
          tres, Iowa City, Iowa
    1990 "Parameters. Perimeters. An Exhibition of
          Sculpture Framed by Language and Time,"
          State of Iowa Historical Museum,   Des
          Moines, Iowa

Yoder, Martha

Parnell, Iowa
Born: 1945, Aberdeen, Idaho
Printmaker

Education: B.A., Bethel College
            M.A., M.F.A., University of Iowa

Selected exhibitions:
    1997 Rock Island Fine Arts Exhibition, Augustana
          College, Rock Island, Illinois
    1994 Bucknell University, Lewisburg, Pennsylvania
    1990 Eve Drewelowe Gallery, University of Iowa, Iowa
          City, Iowa

Beaded Yoke, 1997.
beadwork on cloth
30" x 14"

Young Bear, Mary E.
Tama, Iowa
Born: 1959, Denver, Colorado
Printmaker, beadworker, dollmaker

Education: Study at Marshalltown Community College, Coe College

Selected exhibitions:
1997 "Six Hands, Three Visions," Marshalltown Community College, Marshalltown, Iowa
1997 "Showing Off," Central Iowa Women's Caucus for the Arts, Cedar Rapids Museum of Art, Cedar Rapids, Iowa
1995 MacNider Art Museum, Mason City, Iowa

Wide Lip Mortar II, 1994.
stoneware, mixed media
10"H x 19"W x 19½"D

Zirkle, Merle Waller
Grinnell, Iowa
Born: 1934, Oxford, Michigan
Ceramic sculptor

Education: B.A., University of Mississippi
M.F.A., Southern Illinois University

Selected exhibitions:
1997 Rock Island Fine Arts Exhibition, Augustana College, Rock Island, Illinois
1996 "Mortars and More III," Grinnell College, Grinnell, Iowa
Solo exhibition
1994 "Iowa Artists," Des Moines Art Center, Des Moines, Iowa

Safe Haven: Dragonflies, 1995.
handmade paper
10"H x 19"W x 19½"D

Zmolek, Gloria
Cedar Rapids, Iowa
Born: 1951, Ames, Iowa
Papermaker

Education: B.A., M.A.T., University of Iowa

Selected solo exhibitions:
1997 "Relativity," Henry Nohr Gallery, University of Wisconsin
1995 "Paperworks," Tarrytown, Austin, Texas
1994 Smithsonian Craft Show, Washington, D.C.

Marianne Abel

Cedar Falls, Iowa
Born: 1953, Flushing, New York
Freelance editor/writer and gardener

Education: B.A., University of Pennsylvania
              M.A., University of Pennsylvania

Selected publications:
- 1998 "Ceramics with Four Hands: A Dialogue with Johnny Rolf and Jan de Rooden," *Ceramics: Art and Perception*, June 1998
- 1995 Introduction, *Farm Wives and Other Iowa Stories*, Marianne Abel, ed., Mid-Prairie Books, Parkersburg, Iowa
- 1995 "Celebrating the Art of Taking Risks: Bill T. Jones and Cedar Arts Forum," *Des Moines Sunday Register*, 12 November 1995

Marianne works as a freelance editor/writer and market gardener on the farm she owns and operates with her husband in rural Cedar Falls. She served as editor of the literary and visual art quarterly *Iowa Woman* from 1990 to 1995, and her feature writing in the arts and humanities has been published internationally.

Marianne Abel and "Goldie", Cedar Falls, Iowa 1997

Patricia "Paddy" Blackman

Davenport, Iowa
Born: 1946, Chicago, Illinois

Education: B.A., University of Iowa
              Postgraduate work at University of Hawaii, University of Iowa, Western Illinois University

Selected publications:
- 1995 *Iowa Woman* Magazine, essays
- 1992 "Missing," *Courage in Evidence: Essays and Stories*
- 1989 *Running Home: An Across Iowa Journal*, co-authored with Jennifer Figge

Paddy lives with her family in Davenport where she both teaches and studies writing and literature. She is active in the Quad Cities, where she was charter member and director of River Action, Inc., chair of Family Resources, Inc., has served on the Domestic Violence Advocacy Council, is a member of the City of Davenport Levee Improvement Commission, as well as taking part in many other community activities.

Paddy Blackman, Davenport, Iowa 1998

Carol Lauhon

Bettendorf, Iowa, and Iowa City, Iowa
Born: 1943, Ann Arbor, Michigan
Ph.D. candidate in English, University of Iowa

Education: B.A., Kalamazoo College
              M.A., University of Michigan, Ann Arbor
              M.A., University of Iowa

Selected publications:
    1996   "Focusing on Artists," essayist and essay
            editor, Arts Iowa City exhibition with Robbie
            Steinbach
    1994   "Lessons in Killing Wonder," *The Critical
            Response to Tillie Olsen*, Nelson and Huse,
            eds. Greenwood Press, Westport,
            Connecticut
    1991   "Soul of the Home," *Iowa Journal of Literary
            Studies*, Vol. 11

Carol Lauhon, Iowa City, Iowa 1998

Carol teaches writing and literature at the University of Iowa where she is pursuing a doctorate in English. Her research interest is in nineteenth-century writing by American women. She is also a Quad Cities activist for reproductive rights and family planning. She lives in Bettendorf and Iowa City.

Marjorie Myers

Bettendorf, Iowa
Born: 1940, Liberal, Missouri
Founder and former owner of Vicomm, Inc., a graphic
            design firm

Education: Studied fine art at the University of Missouri
              Commercial art and photography in work-
              shops and seminars

Marge returns to fine art following retirement from over twenty years in the commercial art world. She and her husband reside near the Mississippi River surrounded by woods, wildflowers, and weeds, her favorite photo subjects. She has three grown children, four grandchildren, and enjoys the job title of "Granny" tremendously.

*Marge Myers with daughter, Jo, and granddaughter, Annie,
Bettendorf, Iowa 1997*

*"Emulsional Support Group"
l. to r., Marge Myers, Paddy Blackman, Marianne Abel,
Robbie Steinbach, Carol Lauhon*

Dawn Bowman

Grinnell, Iowa
Born: 1958, Benson, Arizona
Writer

Education: B.S., Iowa State University
B.A., Upper Iowa University

Selected publications:
Series on Vietnam War veterans and Agent Orange.
Feature articles in *The Grinnell Magazine*
Series on diabetes and research by University of Iowa College of Medicine researchers and physicians.

Jean Florman

Iowa City, Iowa
Born: 1952, Washington, D.C.
Writer

Education: B.A., Cornell University
M.A., University of Arizona

Selected publications:
Moments in Iowa History book
Articles in *Country Home* magazine
Articles in *The Iowan* magazine

Harriet Harmelink

Bettendorf, Iowa
Born: 1936, Northwest Iowa
Homemaker, teacher, caterer

Education: B.A., Central College

Selected publications:
Courage in Evidence
Imaging Quad Cities Women Artists, Davenport Museum of Art catalog

Laura Julier

Lansing, Michigan
Born: 1952, New York City, New York
Associate Professor

Education: 1988, Ph.D., University of Iowa

Selected publications:

1995   "Us and Them: A Cautionary Essay about Restructuring Power in the Classroom," *Diversity: A Journal of Multicultural Ideas*, Fall 1995.

1994   "Private Texts and Social Activism: Reading the Clothesline Project," *English Education*, December 1994.

1998   "Voicing the Landscape: A Discourse of Their Own," with Paula Gillespie and Kathleen Blake Yancey, in *Feminist Cyberscapes: Essays on Gender in Electronic Spaces*, S. Kristine Blair and Pamela Takayoshi, eds. New Directions in Computers and Composition Studies Series. Gail Hawisher and Cindy Selfe, eds. Ablex, 1998.

Kay Kehoe

Born: 1918, Ottosen, Iowa
Died: 1996, Davenport, Iowa
Housewife, writer
Education: B.A., University of Iowa

Selected publications:
1993 *Imaging Quad Cities Women Artists*, Davenport Museum of Art catalog, Davenport, Iowa

Denise Lamphier

Grinnell, Iowa
Born: 1966, Waterloo, Iowa
Writer, editorial director at Grinnell College

Education: B.A., Upper Iowa University
M.A., University of Iowa

Selected publications:
The Grinnell Magazine and other publications at Grinnell College
Working on a novel at present

Julie Jensen McDonald

Davenport, Iowa
Born: 1929, rural Audubon County, Iowa
Writer, teacher

Education: B.A., University of Iowa

Selected publications:
Amalie's Story
Pathways to the Present
Ruth Buxton Sayre, biography

Teresa Ruzic

Davenport, Iowa
Born: 1955, Davenport, Iowa
Operations assistant, Family Museum of Arts and Sciences, Bettendorf, Iowa

Education: B.A., St. Ambrose University
M.A., University of Illinois, Springfield

Selected publications:
On Stage magazine
Arts Beat magazine
American Youth Museums newsletter

Index of Photographic Portraits